The
Girnin' Gates

(Where Lions Weep)

Ernest Hume

An Autobiography of
My Boyhood Years

Copyright © 2010 Ernest Hume
All rights reserved. Printed in the USA.
Daisy House Publishing Company
London, Ontario.
ISBN 0-929136-22-5

Oh, unhappy human kind,
In those grim gods, your own creation,
What anguish for yourselves you find,
For babes unborn, what tribulation!

Lucretius

Nemo Me Impune Lacessit

No One Harms Me with Impunity

(National Motto of Scotland)

PREFACE

A full autobiography, as David Hume has said, cannot be written without vanity. For that reason this great philosophical writer produced the shortest autobiography I have ever read. Unlike him, I have no fear of vanity, for there is little of myself to be vain about. *Au contraire*. Then I think, given my litany of failures despite a plethora of talent, would I not fall under the spell of anti-vanity? Is there not a danger that I would take false pride in all the things I had hoped to do as a child, but never did? But, if I had neither succeeded nor failed at anything, what would there be to write about? In that eventuality, this work would end right now. Yet it goes on, for I am reminded of my own Taoistic philosophical reflections which embody the idea that without failure, there would be no success.

In truth, my reluctance to write a full biography is based primarily on the reality that no one, save perhaps my wife and a descendant or two, would want to read it. Who cares about the man who almost climbed Mount Everest or wrote a hundred unpublished novels or who invented the wheel unaware that some Sumerian had done that 10,000 years ago! I fear my minute audience provides little motivation for me to write a work even as humble as David Hume's ten-page autobiography.

But, there is yet another obstacle. To write an autobiography one has to revisit experiences, some of which may be painful. Never a masochist, I find that idea distasteful and a strong deterrent to such an undertaking. Moreover, certain attitudes and beliefs fall in and out of fashion. The vigourous discipline of my childhood, may or may not be characterized as child abuse today. Just as the treatment of recalcitrant children today may or may not have been viewed as pampering and spoiling in the past.

Overriding my objections, my dear wife, Sheila, feels that I should write about my life, now in its seventy-sixth year. So I will write something, but I will confine it to the childhood memories of my childhood time. This boils it down to an account of the life and times of a Scottish boy.

Note that, while I believe that every event described in this work is true, I cannot vouch that they are all in the correct sequence.

Ernest Hume,
London Ontario.

CHAPTER ONE

It was the worst of times.

On October 29, 1929, the stock market crashed. Millions were thrown out of work. Thousands were ruined. Hundreds killed themselves. This was the start of the Great Depression. During the next several years, people would struggle to get by, taking any job they could find, sleeping in flop houses, lining up at soup kitchens, suffering humiliations they never even conceived of before.

This was also the end of the Jazz Age, the Charleston, the speakeasies and the growth in wealth so easily acquired. Almost everyone who was anyone owned stock, often worth hundreds of thousands of dollars, pounds, even yen. They did not need much money. By buying on margin, they were only required to put up 50% of the cost. They could, in appearance, double their assets overnight. Those short on cash could mortgage their property or borrow from the bank. Almost anyone could be paper rich. Stocks rose and rose and rose. The mere actions that people were buying, on margin or not, kept the demand high and stock prices spiralling upwards. One would be a fool not to take advantage. Never mind that they were overpriced. Never mind that most of the buyers were amateurs. Never mind that the price/earnings ratio was ridiculously low.

Then suddenly, it was over. Brokers began demanding full payment. Investors had to sell their stock to make those payments, sending the stock into a free fall. Bankers started calling in loans. Borrowers could not pay. Bankruptcies followed. Property changed hands. Even fully funded investors panicked and sold their stock at enormous losses.

Stocks, good and bad, fell one after the other like a house of cards touched by a nervous, uncontrolled hand. Nothing could keep them from falling. The more they sold, the more the prices fell until, in many cases, they became worthless.

When the dust settled, the hard times began.

Without money, without profits, corporations laid off tens of thousands of workers. To find work in America, which was especially hard hit on account of their longstanding worship of money, Americans travelled everywhere, while in Britain they mostly queued at long lines hoping there was a job at the end of it. Men rode the railways, often risking their lives to find a place with work. Hobos abounded. "Brother, can you spare a dime?"a song sung by such renowned singers as Rudy Vallee, Bing Crosbie and Al Jolson became the hit song of the era.

Few would have anticipated the horror of war soon to come, the wholesale slaughter of men, women and children, the Holocaust, and the violent deaths of some 70 million people.

Yet, all over the world, poor people, stubborn people, continued to dance and make merry and shut out the reality of their existence. Saturday night in particular was a time to party. "I Belong to Glasgow," written and sung, by the great Scottish music hall comedian, Will Fyffe, with the words:

> *I'm only a common old working chap*
> *as anyone here can see,*
> *But when I get a couple of drinks*
> *on a Saturday*
> *Glasgow belongs to me.*

became one of the great party songs of all time. Dance bands flourished everywhere. The young went there, the looking and the lookers. In the United States, prohibition, which was imposed in 1920, finally came to an end. Britain had lamely urged drinkers to sign a pledge of abstinence, usually catching them as they staggered out of a pub at closing time. But, one way or another the merriment continued.

Le Roi Jazzband was a product of these times. Flemming was on piano, Fairley on violin and Hume on drums. Sometimes the latter, who formed the group, would lend his voice and croon to the Clydebank Saturday night crowd. Those were great years for Willie Hume, who had the blue eyes of Harry James and the complex rhythms of Gene Krupra. Moreover, with his good looks, topped by a mop of dark brown hair and an easy outgoing fun-loving personality, he was popular, especially with the girls. These turned out every week to enjoy the music and hoped to be picked up for a dance by someone they liked.

Though a drummer by night, during the day, Willie worked as a machine inspector at Singer Manufacturing Company. But his first love was playing the drums in his own band. He also played for others, for he was a registered member of the Musicians' Union. When he had money, he loved to spend it. When he and friends went to eat or drink, he was usually the first to pick up the bill. Drinking for him meant hot Iron Brew or white coffee. Unlike his father, Pa, and brothers, certainly Jack, he could not abide hard liquor. He tried it once and became so sick that he never wanted to try it again.

Singer's opened in 1884 at Kilbowie, Clydebank on a 46-acre site. The floor area was nearly one million square feet and 7,000 workers were employed producing, for a time, an average of 13,000 machines a week. It was the largest sewing machine factory in the world. More amazing was the fact that it came to employ some 11,000 workers from a population of only 45,000. Singer's was indeed the heart and soul of the economy of Clydebank. My parents worked there and almost everyone knew someone who did.

But Clydebank was doubly blessed. John Brown and Company was another major source of employment for the people of Clydebank. Perhaps one the greatest shipbuilding companies of all time, they built, among many other ships, the Lusitania, the Queen Mary, the Queen Elizabeths (I & ll) and the Empress of Britain employing some 6,000 workers. Both my grandfathers worked there. But the depression hit both of them. Layoffs became more frequent. John Brown, in the process of building the greatest ship ever built, the Queen

Mary, stopped work for three years in 1930. In the early 30s, life in Clydebank was grim. It was no time for marriage. It was no time for children. But it was always time for fun.

* * *

William (Willie) Bell Hume, the son of John Brown Hume—no relation to the shipbuilding magnate— and Mellisa Resa Hume (nee Henry) was born a leo, two months premature at 80 Second Avenue, Clydebank on August 14, 1904, at 1:10 a.m. All together, his mother, bore ten children, five boys and five girls. I would never know my grandmother, Mellisa, for she died two years before I was born. She had her first child in 1893, when only 20 years-old. She then went on to have surviving children in 1896, 1899, 1902, 1907, 1909, 1911, 1912, 1914 and 1915. Despite the strain, she lived to see her 58th birthday.

Of the boys, only John, called Jack, was William's elder. His other brothers were James called Jimmy, Robert called Bertie, Daniel called Joe suggesting more than a touch of indecisiveness or ready-made aliases, just in case. Apart from one Carbeth wartime visit by Uncle James, I knew little of my father's brothers with the exception of Uncle Jack.

I knew his sisters even less. One, Mellisa named after her mother, born in 1899, lived only to be two. The others were Beatrice, Margaret called Peggy, Mellisa, the second one so named, Nancy and Esther. I only ever came to know the last two, and then only slightly.

Though John Brown Hume, known as Pa Hume, worked steadily at John Brown's, his income was sorely stretched to provide food and shelter for such a large family and so the older children were expected, not only to fend for themselves, but to contribute, as best they could, to the whole family.

As a schoolboy reaching for his books, young William, who they all called Willie, knocked over a pot of boiling water that permanently scarred a large area of the skin on his right shoulder and back. Skin grafts were not even considered, and that accident was only one of the many misfortunes he had to endure in his life. The lost time from school and the pressure to make money led to his quitting school after grade eight. He subsequently drifted into various jobs, including a stint as a steward on a Cunard liner crossing to America, but with Pa's help (Pa was a high-ranking Freemason), he eventually got a job at the sewing machine company. But it was music he loved and pursued.

Somehow he acquired a professional drum set, on which he practiced daily. Being gifted with a strong sense of rhythm, he soon became proficient enabling him to perform to a professional standard. Drumming became the centerpiece of his life and a major source of income.

*   *   *

Born on March 11, 1912, Mary Miller Moore was from a respectable Clydebank family. Her father, Thomas Moore, was a foreman at John Brown's Shipyard and a sober steady man— aside from a tipple on a Saturday night. Big Tom, as he was called, was also a die-hard conservative. During a strike, he ignored the name calling and the stones, pulled up his six-foot frame, and resolutely crossed the picket lines. He wanted nothing to do with unions.

He had been born in County Antrim, in Northern Ireland. But he so despaired of the endless pain and poverty of that place, and the "troubles," that he left his home for Scotland where he met and married a Scottish lady, called Jemima Gardner. This proved to be a solid relationship and ultimately an enduring marriage. They had five children, two boys and three girls, though one of the girls, Sissy, died young. Mary was the youngest and much favoured and probably spoiled by her father for she was a pretty girl. She was also clever and completed her high school years with no difficulty. Her elder sister, Jean, had good cause to be jealous, but was of such good heart that she readily forgave any real or imagined slights, and they lived together in relative peace.

When the depression hit Clydebank, their eldest son, Thomas, Jr., following his father's example, left his homeland and travelled to America to seek work. With the depression unabated, it was a struggle there also. At one point, he returned and set up a petrol (gas) station, which did not do well and so he eventually returned to America to work for the rest of his life as a toolmaker and foreman, only returning to Scotland at age 66 to spend his retirement, which lasted some twenty-five years.

Their second son, another Willie, ran away from home and joined the Merchant Navy. That was to be his life until his ship was torpedoed by the Germans, during World War ll, off the coast of Newfoundland. He had joined the Canadian Navy by then and lived in Verdun, on Montreal Island in Quebec. All of big Tom Moore's children eventually found their way to Canada or America.

*   *   *

Dancing was one of the few social activities

that attracted all the young men and women of the day. Mary certainly enjoyed it. Every Saturday night she would head to the dance hall with her friend for an evening of fun and excitement. With Willie on stage, virtually everyone knew him. Eventually he noticed my mother and danced with her. Soon they looked forward to seeing each other every week. The relationship of William and Mary blossomed and they began to meet after the dance.

When word got out, and Big Tom learned of it, he was appalled. It is not likely that he knew about Willie's marriage to Lilias, at least in the beginning. Regardless, he did not hesitate to voice his disapproval of Mary's relationship with Willie. He considered the Humes of Second Avenue irresponsible socialists, the scum of the earth. Moreover, they had a reputation of being somewhat wild.

Regardless, Mary soon became emotionally entangled with Willie who was passionately in love with her. Willie found so many excuses to "inspect" the machines in Mary's department, especially Mary's, that he was reprimanded and might easily have lost his job. His enthusiasm for life, his easy outgoing manner seemed to complement the reserved and demure Mary. He was to her an irresistible enticement into the wild exciting world of living, moving people. This was a far cry from the diet of John McCormack records, which her father played in the leisure hours at their quiet home in Radnor Street.

In the early hours of Sunday, January 29, 1933, William and Mary's relationship culminated in the conception of the illegitimate creature that was to be me. This would not be a virgin birth.

On that same Sunday, far away, in the German Fatherland, Adolf Hitler who was born on April 20, 1889 and his supporters were celebrating his impending appointment as Chancellor of Germany and the beginning of the Third Reich. His chief, and ever loyal supporter, was Dr. Joseph Goebbels, born on October 29, 1897. Together they would truly shock and awe the world.

William and Mary celebrated their love, not knowing that they would pay a terrible price.

CHAPTER TWO

It must have been a shock for my mother to learn that she was pregnant. There were no pregnancy tests available in those days. So she would learn the natural way, a delayed or missed menstrual cycle. It is most probable that she kept it to herself for sometime. To tell her mother was to tell her father whom she knew would be outraged. After all, he had warned her about associating with that man. The only other ear she had available was her older sister Jean who was unlikely to be sympathetic. At the first opportunity she most certainly told Willie, and the news must have taken all the wind out of his sails. He knew, even if Mary was yet to learn it, that he was already the father of a child! So for some time the joy of their love was tempered by its complexity and the weight of growing responsibility.

Of course, eventually, she was forced to tell her family. It must have been very disappointing news for her parents. And if, at that time, they also learned that Willie was already married, Big Tom must have been beside himself.

But there was nothing they could do. Although it would have been an effective solution, abortions were practically unheard of in those days, certainly not among respectable people. The standard solution was to send the wayward daughter away to have her baby and then give it up for adoption. And if Willie harboured doubts about their relationship, this would likely have been the chosen route. He was, however, determined to marry my mother and legitimize the birth. She too wanted to be married and so they decided to ride it out come what may. But that was going to take quite a while.

In the meantime, Mary had no option but to carry on working. At first that was easy for no one would have suspected Mary of fornication. She was not a wild one. She was quiet and conservative, not one you would ever expect to get herself into trouble. But eventually, people would notice. Skinny by nature, there was no chance to hide behind a fattening body. Her stomach said everything.

* * *

As an embryo, I did not even have an unconscious awareness of my being. But as days grew into weeks, I began to feel the forces of my environment. After all, my mother was living in extremely stressful circumstances. Under constant stress, shame, loneliness and no doubt a goodly measure of depression, her body inevitably conveyed this to me. This did not bode well, for a fetus exposed to the stress hormones of its mother may become hyperactive or, lethargic and temperamental in later life. It was certainly not the path to normalcy.

In ways beyond description, I felt the sadness and shame of my mother. However, having now begun the process of forming, I was driven to live and make the best of my circumstances. So I survived the crucial, first three months of my existence.

It was a difficult time for Mary. Being pregnant out of wedlock was a serious sin in those days and, at her father's insistence, she had been forced to continue at work. This was a humiliating experience for her. As the pregnancy became obvious, as the fetus grew, so too did her shame.

On top of that she had to deal with the fact that she could not soon marry the father, for she knew that Willie was already married. Her child, if born safely, was destined to be illegitimate. To compound matters, he had already fathered a child, a daughter called Jean, born on September 21, 1930, a Sunday's child. She was never to know her father.

It was in 1929 when Willie met an attractive English school teacher called Lilias Affleck, born in Sutherland, England in 1907. She had come up from England for a holiday. It is unclear where they met, but it was probably on a dance floor. She was only 22 years old. They fell in love and their relationship culminated with their marriage on April 6, 1930. In the spring of the following year, she became pregnant. It is said that she wanted to return to England to be with her own family and friends. Nostalgia is a powerful force especially when you are pregnant. Willie refused to go to England with her and so she left him. She had her baby in Sutherland. Though there was no action to obtain a divorce at that time, they were never to be reunited.

Mary, just before she had her child, moved to the house of a sympathetic relative. As the time grew close, Mary could only bewail her lot. She had been a bright, well-educated, twenty-year-old girl, noted for her good looks, when she met the man who had dramatically changed her life. Yet, he was only half the problem. She was about to become a mother.

*   *   *

I was born at 4:40 p.m. on Sunday, October 29, 1933 at the Glasgow Maternity Hospital in the wing for unwed mothers, the first born of Mary Miller Moore, who lived at that time at 826 Duke Street, Glasgow having left or been forced out of her home in Clydebank. Given all I'd been through, I did the only thing I could do. I cried like a baby.

No doubt a symbol of their serious intent, I was named Ernest. The problem was that I could not be named Hume. But I was given the next best thing, my mother's surname, Moore. And so, without further embellishment, I was entered into the registrar of births as a boy named Ernest Moore.

Apparently, I had no obvious congenital problems. So everything was deemed to have gone well. The problem now became: what was one to do with me? Mary was in a quandary about what to do next. She knew her parents had no desire to have her return home with an illegitimate baby. The gossip would ruin Big Tom's stout reputation as a careful conservative man. How then could he father such a wayward child? So arrangements were made to place me in the hands of a foster mother. Said to be in someway related to the family, I never did learn who this woman was. Secretiveness was the order of the day. Consequently, I have no idea whether she was married or single, old or young, had other children on not. Most certainly, she would have had a tremendous influence in my development during this early crucial period of life.

I was not totally abandoned. Though my father rarely, if ever, saw me, my mother would take a streetcar to visit me once a week. It is most unlikely that I saw her as my mother at that time. She was just a woman who appeared now and then. My foster mother, who nursed me, spoke to me and played with me daily was the only important person in my universe. And she would remain so for the first year and a half of my life.

But babies are resilient— with support and attention from loving adults, they can adapt to any situation. In fact, a strong, secure attachment to a nurturing adult is a necessary protective biological function, helping a growing child withstand the ordinary stresses of daily life. Given the circumstances this role could not possibly be played by my biological mother. However, in time, after many visits, her face would become familiar and I would have come to trust her.

But my mother's troubles did not end there. In the cold of winter, she now had to go back to her job in the factory and deal with the stares of her fellow factory workers. The bold ones would almost certainly have asked her what had happened to her baby. And given the times, many may have scorned her or indulged in disparaging remarks. She was, one way or another, constantly reminded that she had borne an illegitimate child. There is no doubt that she had no wish for a child under these circumstances. If only she had not had the bad luck of becoming pregnant. The thought must have passed through her head many times, for without the baby, there would have been no humiliation, no embarrassment, no insurmountable problems. But with passionate love, there was no such thing as safe sex. That's why fornication was something that was kept secret, until the "hard evidence" brought it to light.

Oblivious to the world, I did not know that the Vatican state secretary Eugenio Pacelli (later Pope Pius XII) signed an accord with Hitler. Or that the brilliant mathematician, Albert Einstein, arrived in the United States, a Jewish refugee from Nazi Germany. Or that earlier in the month, Germany withdrew from the League of Nations.

Few in Clydebank did.

CHAPTER THREE

In April of 1934, work began again on the great Cunard liner "Queen Mary," at that time the largest passenger ship ever built. She was to be 1,000 feet long, with 12 decks and carry 2,000 passengers. This did much to alleviated the unemployment situation in Clydebank, for those with the right skills. Others still struggled to feed and clothe themselves.

Somehow, during all this miserable time, my mother kept her relationship with Willie going. Being an honourable man, or a man deeply in love, Willie struggled to raise the funds required for a divorce. In the midst of a depression, with work a scarce commodity, it was almost impossible for him to generate the funds to pay for the divorce. He barely had enough money for food. He is also said to have stinted even here, no doubt undermining his immune system, though that concept was not a part of people's lives in those days. The prospects of a happy resolution seemed far away, and time moved so slowly.

Throughout the spring and summer of 1934, I learned, ate and slept each day with no conscious thoughts or memory. Psychologists tell us, however, that our minds are hardly empty. Every little incident, every experience is tucked away someplace in the brain. The taste of food, the sound of music, the sight of objects, the feel of clothes, the smell of cooking all drifted through my growing brain. It was the way of nature. But I was oblivious. Tigers have mothered piglets, cats have mothered skunks, dogs have mothered rabbits. They do not seem to have been conscious of the difference, certainly at the beginning. However, I doubt a pig could ever take on the characteristic of a tiger.

My first birthday arrived with little fanfare and no progress in the situation. Still, I must have served as a reminder of their irreversible transgression. Faced with the fact that, a year after my birth, my parents remained unmarried, could hardly be a cause for any meaningful celebration. The iron grip of poverty was crushing my childhood. But while Britain and America fretted over their unemployment, Adolph Hitler began expanding the German army and navy. More ominous was his planned task of creating of an air force, the Luftwaffe, all in violation of the Treaty of Versailles.

For my part, I continued with the task of surviving.

*   *   *

There seems little doubt that I was a crying infant. The only picture extant of me, where I was clearly less than a year old, I appear to be crying and in some distress. The frown in my face spoke volumes as to how I felt. My eyebrows were knitted. My look, sullen. Since photographs in those days were rarely taken, the photographer must have long waited in an attempt to photograph me in the best possible light, but I was obviously unable to accommodate him even with a smile, never mind laughter. Where I was is a mystery, but I was dressed in what seems to be a Christening robe. It's a moot point, but it is hard to believe that the Church of Scotland would allow the baptism of an illegitimate child with only one legal parent who did not even have physical custody of the child and had no record of being a church goer.

No doubt my foster mother rocked me back and forth to calm me and in time I learned to suck my thumb or indulge in some similar activity to calm myself. When an adult face appeared about 18 inches directly in front of mine, I saw their eyes. As this occurred repeatedly throughout the day, I grew familiar and comfortable in the presence of that person. It would have been surprising if this attachment was not mutual.

More often I stared at things without comprehension, bright lights, a movement, a sound often caught my attention. Visitors, unfamiliar faces, different voices unnerved me. And I could only be comforted by the face, the arms, the warmth of the one I knew. Feeding time was especially important to me. This always brought a familiar, comforting face and, I'm sure, a sound sleep afterwards. Since my mother was in no position to breast feed me, it may have been a wet nurse. More probably, it was a bottle of goat's milk or some such high-fat concoction proffered by my foster mother. This woman would also have had the dubious task of changing my diapers.

As is normal, during my first year of life, I developed a bond of love and trust with my foster mother. The first year of a baby's life may be the most important as it builds its repertoire of sights, sounds, taste, touch and feelings. There is no evidence that I benefited from an association with other children.

Entirely unnoticed in the greater world was my first birthday. Though I hardly knew it at the time, it was the beginning of my struggle to know who I was. But my parents knew. I was a grim reminder of their transgressions.

In the greater world, still deep in depression, such notables as John Dillinger, Bonnie and Clyde, Al Capone, Charles "Pretty Boy" Floyd, "Baby Face" Nelson and Geoge "Machine Gun" Kelly dominated the pages of American newspapers in the year 1934. Violent, arrogant, despicable, they were the talk of the town. Some, like Dillinger, were seen as a modern day Robin Hood.

Largely unnoticed, was the appointment of Heinrich Himmler as head of all the police forces in Germany. But the most significant event was when Hitler became head of state as well as Chancellor. From now on, he would be known as the Führer of Germany or simply the Führer.

At that time, the people of Clydebank had no idea how significant that was. They still struggled to put food on the table.

CHAPTER FOUR

For the first half of 1935, as far as I know, everything stayed the same. I remained in the care of my unknown foster mother, while my biological mother came to visit me when the opportunity arose. Then suddenly the winds of change swept over me leading me to new and unknown environments.

My father's divorce was finalized, paving the way for him to marry my mother. They were married June 28, 1935 at Boquhanran Manse, Albert Road, Clydebank by Alexander Philp, minister of the Boquhanran Parish Church in Clydebank. But neither had any real ambition to return to Clydebank. Together, they rented a room probably in Duke Street and my parents were able, at last, to collect their son, now one and a half years old.

To save money for the divorce, my father had camped out, living in a tent and eating only enough to survive. Living in a tent, for more than a few days, in a rainy country like Scotland is neither a pleasant nor a healthy experience. Inevitably, my father came down with bronchitis that he tried to fight off for many weeks. That enormous scar on his back from the scalding water of a toppled kettle could hardly have helped. Eventually, the worsening symptoms forced him to see a doctor who diagnosed his condition as a serious case of pleurisy and told him to go home and rest. Weeks passed without any significant relief. Another visit to the doctor led to an x-ray. The results were devastating. Both lungs were infected. My father had fallen victim to the "white man's plague," tuberculosis.

The grief that swept over the lives of William and Mary cannot be imagined. My mother was now trapped by a helpless child and a sick husband. Willie had to leave his job at Singers, receiving a polite letter, expressing sorrow for his circumstances and assuring him there would be a job for him whenever he returned. Unable or unwilling to return to work, my mother struggled to live on social assistance.

At that time, tuberculosis was virtually a death sentence. It had claimed the lives of many great Scotsmen such as Robert Burns, Sir Walter Scott and Robert Louis Stevenson. Penicillin, discovered by Alexander Flemming, another Scot, had yet to be proclaimed the wonder drug it was, and although mass produced in the early 1940s it was used primarily for the troops. It would not become generally available until after the war. Too late for my father.

The best treatment in his time was to spend a year in a sanitarium. And so he was sent into exile. Fortunately, it was not far away, for he was sent to one in the Ochil Hills, one of the healthiest areas in Scotland just four miles from Kinross, close to Loch Leven with the Moors of Kinross nearby. Moreover, a daily diet of healthy food was provided. All agreed that it was an ideal place to recover from this terrible disease.

Set 800 feet above sea level, the foundation stone for this building was laid in October 27, 1900 and it was to use the newest treatment for tuberculosis called the "open-air system," where patients were encouraged to walk the grounds and breathe in the fresh air. The toast made at the ceremony was, "Success to the Ochil Hills Sanitarium." And for many, it was their salvation. But my father's condition was too advanced. He was never going to recover. Still, I would not see him for another year.

In the meantime, Hitler tore up the Treaty of Versailles and put the German nation on a war footing. His Nazi Party held mass rallies in stadiums throughout the country including such cities as Nuremberg, attracting tens of thousands of patriotic Germans. Though he frightened the world, he restored Germany's pride, building over 1,200 miles of roadway and reducing unemployment to zero.

The world was mesmerized.

CHAPTER FIVE

I began to come out of my comatose state when I was about two and a half years old. My first memory was sitting at a dining room table struggling with a plate filled with pudding. It was grainy semolina pudding grown cold as I nibbled awkwardly at pieces filling my spoon at the constant urging of the woman who sat across from me. Along with these urgings, the woman, who was my mother, was telling me that I would soon be meeting my father. She made it sound exciting, so I struggled to swallow the greyish paste despite a strong desire to spit it out.

We were on the ground floor flat of a tenement building, I was never to see again.

Outside a lorry drew up, and things began to be moved out of the flat. We were moving to a new home. There was talk about street cars and buses, but eventually I was seated with the driver. Just before we left, another woman came to the window of the lorry and offered me some biscuits. There was a finality about everything that I could not understand. Soon I fell back into my coma.

I awoke again the day my father was to arrive and found myself sitting at a table in front of the fireplace in a huge room. It was a room that I would come to know well, but at that time all I could see was the fireplace and some chairs and all I perceived was the presence of my mother.

Suddenly, my father appeared smiling with great warmth and affection. He energized the whole room with his presence from the moment he came through the door. I was speechless, of course, but filled with an odd feeling of expectation. He soon announced that he had brought me a gift. This perked me up even more. He said it was something new and astonishing.

He proceeded to produce some earphones attached to a device inside a box. I could not imagine what it was. He put on the earphones and jiggled a wire in the box. Satisfied, he put the earphones on me. He asked me what I heard. "Nothing" I told him. He took them back, jiggled the wire some more, then put them back on me. Again he asked me what I heard. I repeated that I heard nothing

He said that you must hear something, and asked me to listen carefully. I told him that I heard a hissing sound.

He twiddled the wire again and told me to try again. Finally, I was able to say: "Yes. In the distance. I can hear some music behind the hissing sound."

I never saw the crystal set again.

*   *   *

My bed was a cot placed in the corner of the room. I remember that I did not like it there. Almost every night I was awakened by nightmares. One in particular sticks in my mind. I was being held down on a table while a dentist was trying to pull out my teeth with a pair of pliers. I dreamt this more than once and would often awake filled with fear and crying. I dreaded the day I would ever have to go to a dentist.

There was one occasion when my parents had to go out and leave me behind. They moved my cot to the opposite corner of the room beside a window, which allowed me to look out over Windsor Terrace and down Clarendon Street. They explained that they would not be long and that I would be able to see them from the window. And indeed I did. I saw them walk down Clarendon Street, look back and wave. But when they were out of sight, I felt somewhat apprehensive. It was very quiet. My eyes were glued to the window. They seemed to take an eternity to return. I never did see them return. I must have fallen asleep.

However, on the whole, these were good times for me. I received a lot of attention. I was taken to the "swings," which I enjoyed very much as long as I was pushed. I was supplied with plenty of toys.

My blondish hair was somewhat wavy and my mother made the best of it. With curlers the waves became long elaborate curls, so much so that I looked like a girl, though I did not know it at the time. There is a picture of me taken at a photography studio, called Jerome's. They thought I was so cute and innocent looking that they displayed my photo in the front window of their shop for some time. I doubt that my likeness to the well-known child star called Shirley Temple was coincidental. Fortunately, I was too young to be embarrassed.

My mother treated me like a doll, and was forever fussing with my hair. She liked to dress me up, once in a sailor suit for yet another portrait. Yet oddly, I have no recollection of any affection only attention. Luckily, my features began to change. As I evolved from baby to boy, my face narrowed, my hair darkened and my nose lengthened. The innocence, however, remained and was very real at that time and for many years to come.

Before I knew it, I was a three-year-old enjoying the comforts of childhood and the care of a union of two doting people who were my parents.

Of course, I did not know that Hitler and Mussolini had joined forces. And that their union was to be known fearfully as the Rome-Berlin Axis.

CHAPTER SIX

In May of 1937, Neville Chamberlain became Prime Minister of Britain. He believed that the Treaty of Versailles had treated Germany badly and that there were a number of issues associated with the Treaty that needed to be put right. But it was much too late. Germany had suffered the humiliation of this ridiculous Treaty for 18 years. It was too late now for appeasement. The die was cast and nothing Chamberlain could do would change the inevitable course of events.

Despite numerous war pacts, Britain and especially America stayed largely aloof from the turmoil in Europe. They were even less interested in the fact that Japan was gobbling up parts of

China at every opportunity. In fact, the Japanese captured the capital city, Nanking, and proceeded to murder hundreds of thousands of Chinese. These soldiers of the Imperial Japanese Army also raped thousands of women, by most accounts some 80,000.

Now over three years old, I was enjoying the exploration of my immediate environment and the attention I received from my parents. On Xmas day I awoke to find that I was the owner of a flashy new pedal car. It was beautiful. I had never seen such a car or known of anyone else who had such a car. But the room we lived in was too small for that and I looked forward to driving it down on the street.

Eventually, it was carried down and I began to drive my first car. It was, however, heavier going than I thought it would be. I quickly learned that my legs were not strong enough to propel it to any significant speed. Nevertheless, I revelled in its look, and envisioned myself speeding along the pavement, hair blowing with the wind.

On day, another child came by on a tricycle. It was so fast and manoeuverable that it made me feel like a dressed up slug. Somehow I persuaded the cyclist to try my motor while I tried their tricycle. How I loved that tricycle. I was to use my motor to bate other cyclists for some time to come.

In the end, I became so proficient on the tricycle that I could lean over in a way to cycle on just two of the three wheels.

One of these cyclists was my cousin Nan, daughter of my Uncle Willie who was the closest and the kindest uncle I knew. I have seen a picture of us playing on the street in front of our close in Windsor Terrace. Uncle Willie was my mother's younger brother, a good and loyal friend to our family. He had left the Merchant Navy and was living in Glasgow at the time with his wife, Jenny, and his daughter. Years later, I was to function as best man at her marriage to a man who proved to be a gangster. Later, he was shot many times and thrown from a car on a highway close to Montreal. The news reported that he had survived but he died some days later refusing to name the killers.

During that time we visited Uncle Willie's home and I recall sitting at a child-size table with child-size chairs enjoying a meal with Nan. Possibly, for the first time in my life I was beginning to feel grown up. Two years later, rather than join the British forces, Uncle Willie opted to join the Royal Canadian Navy, where he ended up on a minesweeper, which was torpedoed by the Germans. After spending hours in the North Atlantic Sea, he was rescued, never to sail again.

Though I often harped to have my motor

carried down the three storeys to street level, it was understandably not something my mother was keen to do. So often I would just go out to play on the pavement in front of our home.

On one such occasion I made my first ever friend. Moreover, it was a girlfriend. A year or so older than me, i.e., about four years old, her name was Janis Laidlaw and almost immediately we became fast friends. She lived at 13 Windsor Terrace, which was across the road from me and a few closes nearer to St. George's Road. We must have spent many days and many hours playing with each other, for I never forgot her.

On one memorable occasion, on a hot summer's afternoon we were playing together on the pavement just outside my home. The sun was so hot that it was melting the tarmacadam road surface. We discovered that if we pushed on it, the road would move. So we pushed on it.

In time, the road surface was moved back revealing a soft black tar that could also be moved. And we moved it. And moved it, pulling and pushed in awe of our discovery. Unfortunately, the tar stuck to our fingers. So we wiped them on the ground, the pavement, our clothes, on everything to rid ourselves of the tar. Eventually, it covered our face, our clothes, and our legs. We just could not get it off.

When she called me and I went upstairs to my mother, she was appalled at the mess and tried rubbing it off with soap and water to no avail, Then she hit on the idea of using butter. Sure enough, the butter seemed to dissolve the tar and she was ultimately able to clean me up.

Though the depression hung on, especially in America, 1937 was to be a favourable year for superstars. Among the many notables born that year were Robert Redford, Dustin Hoffman, Morgan Freeman, Jane Fonda, Warren Beatty, Mary Tyler-Moore, Tom Courteney and Shirley Bassey. Britain produced Anthony Hopkins, and Vanessa Redgrave.

Russia recorded the birth of Boris Spassky, who would become the World Chess Champion. Little did I know that one day, while he was the champion, I would play this man a game of chess.

*   *   *

My fourth birthday was upon me and once again, there was to be a radical change in my life.

Even in those days, a family living in one room was not considered healthy. So my parents had applied for a council house. Given my father's health, the application may have been expedited.

Unfortunately, one could not pick and choose, and this council flat was located at 4 Cranhill

Street, in a less than desirable neighbourhood called Blackhill. It had four rooms including a kitchen, a big improvement in space. It was the first home we ever had and proved to be the last. And so we finally settled down into a "normal" family life.

In a cursory way, I was taught, by my father, how to count up to ten and beyond. I was also taught to sing some songs. One in particular sticks in my mind. "It's a Sin to Tell a Lie." This song had a special meaning for my father. Written in the year of my birth, 1933, it starts with the words, "Be sure it's true when you say, I love you." It put into words the feeling my father must have had during which my parent's love for each other was on trial. In time, however, my father became obsessed with the "Sin to Lie," aspect. In fact he spent the rest of his life instilling in me the fear of telling lies.

However, like most fathers, perhaps even more than most, my father wanted me to be a success, make him proud. He knew he would never be able to achieve anything in his life. He had no job with which to grow and barely any education. He had learned basic arithmetic and reading but was unable to tackle the great works of fiction. He was however determined that I would.

His first task was to teach me how to tell the time. He had a book with a clock and movable hands. It was easy to learn the hours, even the half hours and quarter hours. It was not so easy for me to master the minutes. Though often reduced to tears, he persevered until I could tell the time, right to the minute, without hesitation. Later, I became proud of my accomplishment. Indeed, I amazed many visitors. Few four-year-old boys could look at a clock and say it was twenty-three minutes past two, and be right.

Again with ease I memorized all the letters of the alphabet. Words were more problematic. Eventually I learned to recognise "cat" "dog" "mat" "sat" and the like. I also got lessons in geography – my father had a map of the world on the wall of his bedroom – and I well remember him teaching me the mnemonic: "Cheeky little Italy kicked little Sicily into the Mediterranean Sea."

It soon became time for me to go to school. Although, as a rule, a child did not start school until they were five, as I would be five in less than two months after the start of school, I was able to go to school when I was four. So I was taken by my mother to my first school. The name is forgotten. I do remember we had to cross over a canal using a lock as a bridge. It was a little frightening, but I soon got used to it.

Much of my first days in the baby- class was burned into my four-year-old mind. In those days, reading, writing and arithmetic were the priorities. I recall the teacher holding up large cards with a letter of the alphabet on it. She would explain that it was an A or a U or whatever the case may be. Eventually she would just hold up the cards and ask the class what they depicted. Of course, it soon became obvious that I already knew every letter. Even when she mixed the cards, I named every letter without hesitation. They also learned that I could count, tell the time, and spell many three-letter words.

The following week I was moved out of the baby-class into what would be called today, grade one. There I was among equals and blended in like every other child. We sat at small wooden desks which were placed in rows. As was the custom then, the brightest children, usually determined by a test, were seated at the back, while those requiring more individual attention sat at the front.

When my father learned of this, he told me he would buy me the binoculars I always wanted if I got to the back seat. So I think I tried to be as attentive as I could to pass the monthly test of competence. The competition was tough for there were many bright girls and older boys in the class. Nevertheless, I edged up. But it seemed too slow and I really wanted to have these binoculars.

One day, when at school, drinking milk

provided by the school, I was sick to my stomach. Throwing up, I believe. I am not sure how the teacher dealt with this situation but, to get me out of the way, perhaps out of the sight of others, she placed me at the back of the class. When I got home, I told my father that I sat at the back of the class, hoping I would get the binoculars. Sure enough, some days later, he gave me a pair of binoculars. But I was disappointed, for they were not real. They were toy binoculars with very little magnification. Then again, my placement at the back of the class was not that real either.

The talk of the town, if not the world, was the marriage of the Duke of Windsor, a Nazi sympathiser, to Mrs. Wallis Simpson, an American divorcee. Less noticed, but vastly more significant, was China's declaration of war against Japan. Despite the prevailing barbarism, countries, in those days, went to war by politely serving notice with a formal declaration.

CHAPTER SEVEN

During this period, I began to see the rough side of life. Even at five, I often walked home from school by myself, passing through streets where kids ran wild. They scoffed, shouted insults and even threw stones. Needless to say, when on my own, I went home as quickly as possible.

At first I was allowed to drive my pedal motor in the street. But no one else in the neighbourhood had such a motor, so it drew a lot of attention. I did let others drive it but many did not treat it with respect. They would crash deliberately into lamp posts, jump on it or up-end it. When I refused to let someone ride it, I was frequently bullied out of it regardless. Eventually, I stopped taking it onto the street.

Sometimes my father felt well enough to get out of bed, and he would take me to the park. Usually, I went straight to the swings and extolled my father to push me. There were other diversions, huge slides and roundabouts where you had to hold tight for dear life, especially when a big boy pushed it around quickly. You could easily reach the point of being dizzy. But I loved it. And like most kids, I was always trying to persuade my parents to take me to the swings.

On one occasion, we travelled further to a park which had a small lake in the middle. Many people had miniature yachts, perfect models, which they sailed across the lake. Though basically toys, some were two feet long and were properly rigged down to every detail. Men carried long poles with rubber tips which they used to push their boat out onto the lake or divert it, if it was sailing into the side. It was a wondrous sight for me and I have loved yachts ever since.

It was such a popular sport that square wooden platforms were built out into the lake to enable boats to be placed and pushed more readily into the water. Sometimes a strong gust of wind sent a boat racing across the lake. This forced the owner to scramble around the lake to head it off. As these platforms were crowded, people had to elbow their way to the water's edge.

My father stood by as I took it all in. Wanting to get closer to the boats, I worked my small body through the people on the platform, finally getting to the edge where I could see the detailed rigging of these magnificent yachts being launched. Suddenly, I was bumped and fell headlong into the lake. The memory of the water around by face still lingers. Unaided, I would certainly have drowned. But, just as suddenly, I was whipped out of the water by my father who must have raced to save me. I was, of course, soaked to the skin and cold. Then my father did a wonderful thing. He covered me with his jacket, swung me up on his shoulder and marched home. Despite the scare, I felt good about myself and my father.

My interest on boats prompted my father to show me how to make one. He took a piece of paper and folded it in such a way as to make a paper boat with a little pyramid in the middle. At the earliest opportunity I took it outside to test it. Having recently rained, I was able to sail my boat in the water that flowed along the gutter beside the sidewalk. I thought gutters were fascinating places. Only later did I learn that it was the lowest form of achievement. No one wanted to end up in the gutter or have their children called guttersnipes.

Although my mother was always there, she

did not seem to have had any impact on me. She never read to me, played with me or taught me anything that I can remember. She did provide our meals and occasionally took me with her when she went shopping. Even in those days, shopping wore me out, especially when she walked ahead of me and I was forced to labour to catch up.

In Europe, Hitler had sent his troops into Austria and gained control of that country by wearing out its government leaders. Not satisfied with that, he demanded, and obtained, a piece of Czechoslovakia called the Sudetenland.

But, the great event of the year in Scotland was the Clydebank launching of the world's greatest luxury liner, the "Queen Mary" by Queen Mary herself with King George V by her side. It was a moment shared by many of my family, and I was there. There is a picture extant that appears to be of me and my mother with the mighty ship in the background. Certainly, we would have appeared very much like that. Little did anyone suspect that this ship was to play a vital role as a troop carrier in World War ll. It survives to this day as a tourist attraction in the United States at Long Beach, California.

CHAPTER EIGHT

Despite events in Europe, for me, the year 1939 began with an air of tranquility. My mother would take me on visits to see my grandmother and Aunt Jean. Sometimes we stopped for lunch at the City Bakery's Cafeteria. When I went there, I had only one thought in mind. Will I get a chocolate cup? This was a small cake of cream-filled chocolate of which I never grew tired.

Adults, however, had cause to be concerned. Hitler had begun to plan for the invasion of Poland. Most feared that such aggressive action would draw Britain into a war with Germany. And that, they knew, would radically change the dynamics of Europe, if not the world.

My world, too, was about to radically change. My mother broke the news of the coming of a baby to our family. This was surprising news and left me with some bewildering questions. Where do babies come from anyway? I understood what a baby was. But how was it made? A five-year-old has many questions. Blissfully unaware of any change in my mother's physical being, what she told me did not provide the answers that I sought. Finally, when we visited a clinic, a doctor answered my question. It would be made of bottles, he said. But where would it get its nose, I asked him incredulously. He told me that would come from a cork. I had no doubt he was pulling my leg, but it left me uncomfortably ignorant.

In October of that year, I would become six-years-old. Though I could not entertain the thought at that time, my infancy was about to end.

* * *

As the year progressed, the fear of war gripped all of Europe including Britain. German power was a menace to the world. Hitler continued to build his military arsenal with a naval expansion programme specifically powerful enough to crush the Royal Navy, he hoped. He pushed his plan for the invasion of Poland. He signed the Pact of Steel with Italy. Hitler and Stalin agreed to divide Europe between themselves. The conflict was becoming worldwide. In the face of this threat, the United States, and the Scandinavians, *declared their neutrality*. With Russia and America neutralized, Hitler was free to ravage Europe as he pleased.

By August, the concern of the British government reached a new high. Women and children were encouraged to leave the country if they could. Many went to America, which seemed the nearest and most obviously safe heaven. As my Uncle Tom lived there, my parents decided that I too should be sent to America, at least for the duration of the war. I was numbed by the idea, but was assured that it would be safer, and that my uncle would take good care of me.

The necessary papers were prepared, and I was taken to an emigration doctor for a health check up. I distinctly remember a nurse sticking her fingers in my ears and asking me, from behind, if I could hear her speak. I could, and in the end, I was deemed an acceptable candidate to enter America.

Hitler attacked Poland on September 1, 1939. Britain declared war on Germany on September 3. It was then determined that I would be among the first to sail for America at the end of September.

*   *   *

The SS Athenia, built by Fairfields in Scotland, left Glasgow bound for Montreal on September 1 with some 1,400 passengers and crew. It was torpedoed without warning by a German U-boat, the first ship sunk during World War ll. It sank on September 3 about 220 miles west of the Hebrides. A sturdy ship, it took 14 hours to sink, which allowed time to save many lives. Only about 120 people died, but the effect was instantaneous. The plan to send British children to America was cancelled. I was put back on square one. I would not be going to America.

No sooner had all this sunk in than we were swept up by the government's plan to evacuate the children of industrial cities to the country. My mother, who was now about seven months pregnant, and I were herded onto a train and taken to Perth, a quiet town in the heart of Scotland. After disembarking from the train, we stood with hundreds of others, like refuges, waiting to be moved to our living quarters, which in most cases appeared to be barracks or some similar buildings with row upon row of beds. It was not something we looked forward to.

Then, from almost nowhere, a spry grey-haired woman appeared from out of the crowd and spoke to my mother as she looked me over. Then, somewhat baffled, we were led out of the crowd into a large black automobile and taken to a mansion surrounded by beautiful yellow-leafed trees. We had been rescued from the hoi polloi by a lady, whose name I believe was Mrs. Forster. I understood that she was a wealthy widow and owned a chain of tobacco shops. Most certainly, I knew she was kind.

This time in Perth became a very pleasurable period of my life. It was my first glimpse of wealth. We did not eat with her, but we were led by a maid to a dining room with a large table set with white napkins and silver cutlery. I had never seen a napkin before. The downside was that we were not able to fully appreciate the gourmet food we were served. I particularly recall a dish that was covered in white sauce, which neither me nor my mother was bold enough to eat. At the first opportunity, my mother took our plates and washed the food down a nearby toilet. I think we enjoyed the desserts.

The weather was especially warm and sunny and my mother often took me to a nearby park, which had an abundance of flowers. I remember one specific day. It was a joyful summer day, a day of fresh air and sunshine, a day of flowers and freedom to cavort along the paths, around the flower beds filled with myriad unknown flowers. Hopping, skipping, trying to walk along the edges without losing balance, sometimes with arms spread like an airplane, sometimes walking backwards. The trees in the park stood tall and full, laden with leaves that reflected the autumn colours and lazily rustled in the light irregular breeze. I loved to feel the breeze on my face. I loved the trees. I loved the sun. I loved the peace. Everything that day, in the quaint, quiet, Scottish town of Perth was wonderful.

My mother, possibly eight months pregnant at this time, was also tranquil. I jumped around like any happy six-year-old. On one occasion I noticed bees going from flower to flower, One buzzed around me scaring me somewhat for I knew they could sting. But my mother assured me that if you do not bother them they will not bother you.

On top of that, Mrs. Forster was truly kind to me. On more than one occasion we played bagatelle together in that large dining room, setting the board on the table. Her bagatelle board was a work of art and no small toy as it must have been several feet long. I seem to recall that she tried to entertain us with a simple game of cards. And once she let me go and pick some apples from the orchard that was part of the grounds at the back of her house.

She also introduced me to another boy about my age, a grandson, a neighbour, I do not know.

We played happily together and quickly became friends, perhaps the first real friend I ever had, despite the brevity of our relationship, which ended on an unhappy note.

We were playing in the back garden turning around and around until we were dizzy. We then joined hands and began to twirl around and around. Our hands slipped, and I fell on top of my left arm breaking it just above the elbow. And I cried aloud with the pain. Our host sent for an ambulance and I was taken to a local hospital.

Lying on a hospital bed, I recall the doctor placing a cloth lightly over my face, then pouring ether on top, apparently to put me to sleep. But when he asked me if I was asleep, I gave a resounding "no." Minutes later, he placed a bag over my face, and fed me chloroform. I was immediately rendered unconscious. When I awoke, my arm had an Elastoplast-type bandage around it. Then I was fitted with a sling and sent home.

My kindly host insisted that I rest in bed for a while. At mealtime, she sent her maid to me with a tray with what looked like a small teapot. It was soup, I was told. But I was incredulous. Soup comes on plates. Nevertheless, when I sucked on the spout it proved to be tasty soup indeed.

A day or two later, my life was to be changed again.

*   *   *

My mother received a post card informing her that my father was seriously ill. He had tried to paint the house when we were away. But it was too much for him; he had a haemorrhage. On top of this, my unfortunate mother was now in the advanced stages of her pregnancy. There was little choice. We had to return to Black Hill.

There, for the first time in my life, I was put to bed in a room by myself. I remember one night when I just could not sleep. I heard voices from another room. How much I needed it, I don't know, but I called out that I wanted a glass of water. There was no response so I cried out again and again and again as loud as I could. "Mammy, I want a drink of water." I was very troubled and felt very much alone in this strange darkened room. I do not know why I did not get up. I just kept whining, and crying until, at last, my mother came asking me what was wrong. I told her I wanted a drink of water. She got it and I drank it, somewhat appeased. But for the first time, I consciously felt I had been neglected. I did not yet fully grasp that I had lost my importance.

A month after my sixth birthday, a midwife came into my bedroom in our tenement flat in Cranhill Street, Blackhill, to display my newborn sister wrapped in a blanket. "So what do you think she asked?"

"She has no neck," I said staring.

The midwife went on to explain that she was not yet strong enough to hold her head up. That seemed to make sense to me and I asked no other questions, though I stared a while at this helpless, unaware human entity who had come to be my sister.

CHAPTER NINE

During the year 1940, the full extent of Hitler's evil was to permeate virtually every country in Europe. Breaking all the laws and treaties, which held Europe together, Germany invaded Norway, Denmark, Holland, Belgium, and Luxembourg. The Dutch fought fiercely, but after losing a quarter of their forces, 100,000 troops, they surrendered. Soon the Germans controlled Brussels and Antwerp. Belgium was forced to capitulate as did the others. That same year Hitler took Calais, Amiens and finally Paris. Hitler was so jubilant, he had a three-day celebration. His transgressions had been rewarded with inglorious victories and quickly led him to greater transgressions, like looting the art treasures of Europe. Success often breeds greed.

But I had my own troubles. When my sling was removed, we found that the skin between the elbow joint had stuck together preventing me from straightening my arm. My father worked assiduously on this, rubbing on oil, pulling it, making me exercise every day. Bit by bit, the stretch range increased until my arm was straight once more.

My transgressions also seemed to have increased during my stay in Blackhill, most of them worthy of punishment in the eyes of my chronically ill father. I cannot always recall what they were, but I do remember the punishments. On one occasion, he beat me with his belt raising welts and breaking my skin. Of course, I was terrified. But then I vividly remember that, afterwards, he sat me on a kitchen counter top, or table, and patched me up with bandages and Elastoplast. My mother said nothing. I think she thought it was not her place to interfere and she didn't.

While this was going on, one of World War ll's most extraordinary events took place — The Battle of Dunkirk. The massive German army, complete with armour, moved so quickly that it successfully cut off the British Expeditionary Force in France, pinning it against the waters of the English Channel. It was a catastrophic defeat.

Their slaughter was almost certain. But Hitler, oddly, ordered his generals to halt their attack for three days allowing Britain to evacuate what was left of its army. Goering, however, did not stop the relentless attacks by the Luftwaffe.

At the end of May into June, the British sent their warships to evacuate all the soldiers they could. But the effort did not end there. The British people, using every available fishing boat and pleasure craft, risked their lives to cross the rough seas of the Channel to rescue the stranded soldiers, one by one. The Channel was blanketed with small boats coming and going until, finally, the effort was over.

Unfortunately, despite saving almost 350,000 troops, the British were forced to leave behind, 2,000 guns, 60,000 trucks, 76,000 tons of ammunition, and 600,000 tons of fuel, which virtually disarmed its army and left Britain reeling.

* * *

One day, we too were left reeling. My mother became so ill that a doctor had to be called. She was diagnosed with typhoid fever. As this was a highly contagious disease there was some concern that I may have it also. To find out they took a sample of my blood. This was quite a frightening experience as it involved piercing my skin with what seemed to me a huge needle. It hurt and I cried, but I did not have scarlet fever. My mother, though, was taken to be quarantined in a hospital for several weeks. With a sick man and now a baby to look after, we were provided with help in the form of a stern-faced home helper, which changed the tone and the whole dynamics of the house.

The dynamics in Britain's House of Commons had also changed. A coalition government under the leadership of Winston Churchill had taken command. Standing in the House of Commons, faced with this overwhelming defeat, he proclaimed: "We shall defend our island whatever the cost may be, we shall fight on the beaches, we shall fight on the landing grounds, we shall fight in the fields and in the streets . . . we shall never surrender." The Battle of Britain was about to begin.

* * *

With my father almost always in bed, and the home helper occupied with my sister, I was free to run wild. I played on the streets with other wild boys. Being wartime, we were very interested in bombs and found a way to manufacture our own. All one needed was a thick nut and two bolts that fitted the nut. With one bolt screwed partway into the nut, you packed the nut with the sulphurous material from the striking end of a match—we used Swans matches—then screwed in the other bolt. When you threw this into the air so that it fell on a hard surface, it exploded in a cloud of smoke. Moreover, these "bombs" could be repacked and used again.

Another of our favourite games was to jump on the back of a lorry, just as it was taking off, and go for a free ride. As these were local lorries providing goods or services, they would stop frequently enabling us to jump off and on accordingly, though sometimes we had to jump off even as the lorry was moving. We were fearless. The drivers never seemed to notice, but our home helper did and promptly told my father, who taught me another lesson in no uncertain terms.

*　*　*

Hitler was now prepared to invade Britain which, with Europe's countries either conquered or aligned with Hitler, stood alone against Germany's military might. The Battle of Britain began as a one-sided attack by Luftwaffe bombers. But Britain was fully aware that it would succumb if the Germans gained air superiority. So they began feverishly building fighters, the Hurricane and the Spitfire among the most notable. These aircraft, often piloted by Poles, Canadians, New Zealanders, Czechoslovakians and other nationals took on the Luftwaffe's mighty Meshersmitts. They fought fiercely, almost daily, for months. In the end, the British lost 827 aircraft, but they almost destroyed the Luftwaffe by shooting down 2,409 German planes. It was Third Reich's first major defeat. The success in this battle for the skies prompted Churchill to say: "Never in the history of human conflict has so much been owed by so many to so few."

Shortly before my mother returned, my father and I visited her. We were not allowed in the hospital, but my mother was able to climb on top of a high wall as we stood on the street below. She seemed cheerful and rested as they chitchatted. When she did finally come home, the home helper was sent packing. Actually, she may have happily quit.

As the Germans were unable to win air superiority over Britain, they resorted to aerial attacks on its towns and cities. Their main target, for sometime to come, was the City of London. This attack, which began on September 7, 1941, was completely indiscriminate. They "carpet bombed" houses, shops, schools, churches, buildings of every sort that were found in abundance in this vast city.

They began by sending over some 350 bombers escorted by some 600 fighters in the afternoon. For two hours, they rained hundreds and hundreds of incendiary and other bombs on the city. With the city ablaze with fire, the worst since the great fire of London in 1666, they attacked all night, with wave after wave of bombers, until the early hours of the following morning. This was the beginning of what became known as the London Blitz, an attack that was to go on until May 7, 1942 and forever change the nature of war.

Designed to crush morale, weaken resistance as well as destroy factories, it only strengthened the Londoner's resolve. It did nothing to make it easier for the Germans to invade Britain.

Other cities too, including Glasgow were harassed by German aircraft. Planes would come in the dark and drop bombs at random. When they did come, a siren would alert everyone. Once I stood with my father and watched the searchlights scan the sky. You could hear the drone of the German airplanes and the sound of ack-ack guns all around. A flare was dropped and then we thought we saw a searchlight reflect on an airplane. Everything went silent until we heard the sound of a Spitfire chasing after the airplane. Then we retreated to the lower flat of the tenement, where those who lived on the uppers floors waited out the air raid. Even there, on occasion, everyone would grow quiet as we listened to the sound of a whistling bomb, hoping it would not hit us. We also felt safer in the company of other people. And, needless to say, we were all relieved to hear the all-clear siren and to be able to go back to bed.

CHAPTER TEN

Food was always a problem and sometimes we just did not have any. On one such occasion I remember being sent out to buy a lb. or so of tripe, the rubbery lining of a sheep or cow's stomach. Boiled tripe was as tasteless as nettle soup. My father ate it, but I could not for I suspected it would remove whatever food I still had in my stomach.

Though confined to bed most of the time, my father had stuck maps all over the walls of his room, mostly European maps, to follow the war. Now aided by a wireless, he listened to every report on every battle and plotted all the Allied advances on these maps. He became obsessed with the war and on more than one occasion expressed his regret at not being able to fight. He wanted to "die with his boots on" not in bed. But that was not to be.

On the morning of the 14th of March, 1941 there was a knock on the door of our Blackhill flat. With me standing behind, my mother opened the door to reveal my grandma and Auntie Jean standing there with cases in their hands. They looked like they had arisen from the dead for their faces were pale and black with soot. We were stunned.

Starved and exhausted, they explained that they had spent the night in the cemetery, had no food and little sleep. Even as the bombs were falling, they were ordered by a warden to leave their home immediately. They threw some clothes into a suitcase and fled into the street to be directed to the cemetery to avoid the danger of falling buildings.

In the night of March 13, 260 German bombers had flown over Clydebank dropping high-explosive bombs, incendiary bombs and land-mines. For nine hours they pounded the town. Their goal was to destroy the munitions factories and shipbuilding facilities. Instead, for the most part, they destroyed its residential buildings.

Not satisfied, they sent another 200 bombers the following night to drop more bombs for another seven and a half hours. Clydebank was devastated. It was the single most vicious attack made on Scotland. Perhaps, on a population basis, the worst hit town in all of Britain. Hundreds died and hundreds more were injured. Out of the approximately 12,000 houses in the town, only seven remained undamaged. In the end, 35,000 citizens lost their homes including my grandma. Now they stood before us, pale and shaken with nowhere to go. And so, our home became their home.

Their Radnor Street tenement house was still standing when they left, and still was when they returned a few days later to try and rescue some of their possessions. But they were not allowed to enter as the building was in imminent danger of collapsing. Apart from some clothing, all my grandma was able to grab as she left was a clock, given to my grandfather on his retirement, a clock I now have among my possessions.

* * *

Aunt Jean was always willing to take me places. I recall that she once took me to Loch Lomond. This fresh water lake was immortalized in 1841 with the song "The Bonnie Banks o' Loch Lomond." I remember too being disappointed for I had hope to paddle in it only to be frightened off when I walked in. My feet immediately sank into the thick silt along the embankment. Nevertheless, I remember I enjoyed the outing.

Another time, I forget which year, she took me to see the pantomime, Peter Pan. It was my first and last pantomime. Like all the children there, I thoroughly enjoyed it. Like everyone else, I clapped my hands to help bring life back to Tinkerbell. It only puzzled me that Peter Pan was played by a girl. I could not then know the wisdom of its Scottish writer, James Barrie. Peter was not a boy or a girl, but a child who never wanted to grow up. Psychologists know now that the child (Peter Pan), hides wrinkle free in all of us and will until we die.

There was another occasion, when we lived in Blackhill, when my aunt took me out to the park and it had rained. So I returned home with damp cloths and wet hair. My father was beside himself, yelling at Aunt Jean and beating me. Never, she was told, was she to ever take me out again without his permission. Even at that age I understood his motive, he was afraid I would catch a cold that could develop into tuberculosis. An unfounded belief, but his belief, and my mother's, all the same.

But even prior to that incident, my father and aunt did not get on too well. Though it was his right, he often placed restrictions on me that Aunt Jean, not to mention me, did not like. One day my Aunt got permission to take me to the pictures. I was very excited about that. My father, however, insisted that I could not go out if it was raining. And that day it rained. I remember looking out a window forlornly watching the rain bounce in the puddles, hoping it would stop. It didn't.

He seemed to have a better relationship with my grandma. I am sure she was a great help to my mother in looking after my father and sister. I had no responsibilities for her at that time. My self-assigned role was to stay out of my father's way as much as possible, and show up for meals.

But winds of change blew over me again.

*   *   *

One morning Aunt Esther arrived with a car, about two hours later than expected. She was taking us all on a trip to Crief. I recall, like a typical kid, asking repeatedly when are we going to get there. I seemed to me like an eternity. Moreover, when we got there, it was, to me, a quiet, boring place. Everything seemed closed. I was not impressed. Moreover, I took no notice of all the talk that went on among the adults. I probably amused myself, as I often did, daydreaming my time away.

Then something surprising happened. We did not go back to Cranhill Street. Instead we were driven to Whitecrook where a boyfriend of Esther's, called Frank MacLean, had a large flat. Esther was married, but her husband, Fred McMahon, had been called up by the Army and sent abroad. Frank was a postman, an easy going man whose father had been a Postmaster General and had accumulated some degree of wealth. Frank had a kidney problem, which probably kept him out of the army.

More surprising was the presence of other uncles and aunts, all siblings of my father, and their children. Our stay there seemed to develop into one long party. Aunt Esther played the piano using some "vamping" technique she was learning. We all sat around the kitchen while my father told stories and played the principal role in a party game called "Forfeits." In this game, everyone put something belonging to them in a hat, which my father mixed about. He then pulled out an article and the owner had to provide some form of entertainment or forfeit their possession. Some had to sing in one corner, dance in another corner, recite poetry in the third and act like a chicken in the fourth or some such thing. For most, it seemed to be fun. For me, it was an alarming experience. Somehow, despite my distress, I think I was forced to sing a song.

One day, I was playing in a back room with one of my female cousins. I think I was playing doctor and touched her in a private part. But my cousin had no interest in playing the patient. She ran back to the kitchen and told her mother. And of course everyone else who was sitting around would hear about it, including my father. I waited in the room by myself wondering what would happen. After what seemed a very long time, my father, unable to think of a better way to handle it, burst into the room angrily yelling at me for what I had done. Then he went a step further. He grabbed a poker and chased me around the room as I screamed blue murder, which I thought, even at that time, was as much to placate the mother as to punish me. If he hit me at all, there was no physical damage that I remember. But I was terrified.

There was, of course, a lot of adult talk about the war, but I was too young to be part of that. In the end, they apparently decided to move the children out of the town into the country, where my parents were to look after them. So, one day, my mother, father, sister and I were taken by car to a large hut in a place called Carbeth where other cousins were already embedded.   And what a wonderful place that was, a Scottish Shang-ri-la, a paradise, certainly for children such as us. To me, it was a great adventure.

Nearby was a burn (stream) from which my father engineered a swimming hole. We broke down the banks on both sides of the burn so it resembled a pool and we built a dam to deepen the water for swimming. As it was summertime, it got a lot of use.

Across the way, from the front of the hut, was a hill full of ferns and hoards of rabbits, which vanished as soon as I approached to catch one. And not too far away lived two small horses one brown, called Donald, said to be virtually blinded by working in the mines and another sharper smaller white horse called Sheila, his constant companion. We also developed a victory garden in front of the house and grew tomatoes in a homemade hothouse. All summer we waited in vain for tomatoes to appear. Then one day we were all called in to witness a miracle. Suddenly, there were ripe red tomatoes everywhere. I was amazed. Only later did I learn my father had bought them and tied them onto the plants. It certainly fooled me.

Janice and I, along with cousins Madge, John, Margaret, Edith, Eric, were there, as I understood it, to escape any harm from the War. But I thought little of the War then, even when ack-ack guns were mounted on a hill nearby and military convoys frequently passed by on the road in front of our hut. My seven-year-old mind was more concerned with the possibility of wolves in the hills and the lost treasures to be discovered, and we made expeditions along the burn and up into the rocky hills. My companion and leader was my older cousin John Hume, son of James. Together, we made bold excursions into the unknown, armed with sticks and carrying a goodly supply of HP sauce sandwiches.

We were very close at that time, literally and figuratively, for we all lived in one small hut, half of which was for sleeping (it had a double row of bunk beds). The other half was our kitchen/living room, where we ate such delicacies as rabbit and nettle soup. There was no electricity and our water came from collected rain in barrels and a nearby spring. At night, tucked into our bunks in total darkness, my father would tell us ghost stories, our favourites being about vampires.

Things did not always go smoothly for me. I developed bronchitis and was kept in for a time, much to my consternation. More traumatic, however, was an incident which occurred as we all sat around the kitchen table. I let go an uncontrollable sneeze into my plate of soup, which earned a sudden slap across the face from my father. I was devastated. I felt my face burn red, not so much from the slap, but the humiliation. Everyone went quiet.

We all loved it when Aunt Esther came to visit. With characteristic flair, she would drive up in an automobile, slow down, so all of us kids could jump on the running board and get a good hold, and then she would slowly cruise to our little country hut amidst our enthusiastic screams. Also once Uncle James came to visit and although on leave, proudly wore his military uniform. He had, if I remember correctly, been in the tank corps fighting the Germans in North Africa.

After a collective and fruitless effort to smoke out a rabbit—we did chase one out, but it got away—I decided I could do better myself. I often saw rabbits running around the small hill across from our hut and they looked pretty vulnerable to me. They jumped in and out of the many rabbit holes among a sea of ferns. So I gathered some stones and announced that I was going rabbit hunting. I climbed the hill, parked myself in a promising spot and waited and waited. As I was about to quit, a rabbit stuck its head out from a hole right beside me catching me unawares. By the time I was in a position to throw the stone, it was gone. So were my aspirations of being a rabbit hunter.

On another occasion, I was down by the burn, when I noticed a thrush just across from me. I do not know if it was ill or not, but it did not move even although I was just a few feet away. Sensing a chance to get a bird, I threw the head of a golf iron at it. I was shocked when I made a direct hit and ran back to the hut to tell the others. They came and found that the bird was dead. The girls thought it was a terrible thing to do. I felt that I had just killed Cock Robin. Branded a killer, I had to do penance.

We had previously built a graveyard for the trout and other worthy creatures. So it was decided to bury the thrush there, but in a proper funereal fashion. I had to sit by the grave, with a Bible in my hand, and express my sorrow after which, they sang a hymn reducing me to tears.

Those of us over five, went for a time to a school near Carbeth. I recall being proud of the "stars" I received from my teacher for my good work and walking home joyfully singing songs such as "I've Got Six-Pence," though I never had a penny, and "Nine Green Bottles, " which accidentally fell on countless occasions.

Then suddenly, for reasons I did not know, our months long stay in Carbeth ended.

*   *   *

I was transported to yet another world, the relatively urbane world of Drumchapel, then no more than a village. The Carbeth arrangement may

have ended from a falling out between Frank and
Esther. Frank was clearly fond of Esther, but I
suspect that her main interest in him was his
money. In any case, we all broke up and went our
own ways.

My smooth-talking father befriended Frank
Maclean and when Frank bought the house at 17
Golf Drive, Drumchapel, we all went along with
him. My mother became the housekeeper, providing
the meals and so on, while my father looked after
the household affairs. Frank continued his work as
a postman. We never saw Esther.

To me the house was a palace. It had two
bedrooms, a nursery and a bathroom upstairs and
a living room, dining room and a kitchen
downstairs. Moreover, it had a front lawn, a garden
along the side and a huge back garden. My mouth
fell open when I saw a telephone in the house, and
I thought immediately this was a home for wealthy
people. The telephone soon disappeared, however.

Once again I had a room to myself, albeit a
small nursery room. A wide border went all around
the room depicting the characters from "Peter Pan,"
including Captain Hook, the crocodile, Wendy,
Tinkerbell as well as Peter. In the long bright nights
of summer, I often passed the time staring at this
border.

My parents and sister occupied the main

bedroom, while Frank slept in the second bedroom. The arrangement worked well. There was, at that time, peace and balance in the house.

* * *

There was a brick air raid shelter at the far end of the back garden, but most people considered them useless. A bomb could hit an air raid shelter as easily as hit a house. Some had suffered a direct hit killing everyone inside. So, an Anderson shelter was installed next to the brick one. It had the advantage of being largely underground.

One day I climbed up on top of the old brick shelter, which enabled me to look down on the Anderson shelter. It looked to me that I could easily jump over the baffle wall in front of the shelter onto the top. One day I did—and missed. I came crashing down on the concrete edge of the entrance, landing on my chest and slithering down to the space between the entrance and the baffle wall. I lay there in pain for almost an hour afraid to move, afraid to cry out. When the pain abated I limped back to the house. No one ever knew of it.

We built a brick wall at the base of a rockery which divided the back garden. I remember when that was built. A lorry dumped a load of bricks at the front and left us to it. We had to move the bricks from the front to the back. To accomplish this, Frank would throw a brick toward the back where I stood, then I would pick it up and throw it into the backyard. This worked well, until one time when I was turning back for another brick. Frank threw it a little high and it hit me in the side of my brow, almost knocking me out. It bled, of course, and left me with a small scar I never lost.

Frank was good to me, to us all. He put up with me jumping on his back, though my parents were not amused. He also was a keen cyclist and he taught me how to cycle, though my legs could barely reach the pedals. I was quickly becoming taller but, in the beginning, I had to slip my leg under the crossbar to get on the pedals.

For reasons I never knew, my grandpa, (father's father), appeared at the house with a girl called Irene. They stayed for some time for I became friends with Irene, who was several years older than me. For a time, at least, I know she slept with me in the nursery. She was starting or about to start high school, and I remember she could write very well. However, I never really knew who she was.

Pa Hume, as most seemed to call him, never bothered with me. He would leave early in the morning and when he came home, he went directly upstairs. I remember, when in the bathroom washing his face, he would rinse it five or six times with a loud gurgling noise. Once he brought home a present of some sort for Irene, but nothing for me. I think my father was annoyed at this and they quarreled over that and perhaps other things. All I know is that he and Irene left shortly after and I never saw either of them again.

It had been an eventful year. And I was soon to be eight years old.

CHAPTER ELEVEN

Frank was a shy bachelor and my father used to encourage him to go to dances and meet some girls. One day he brought home a woman called Cathy. I remember my father turning on the charm and even kissing her on the cheek as she left. At my father's urging, Frank continued to go out with Cathy and soon they were married. I think she stayed with Frank in his room, but I don't remember seeing her about the house much.

My happiest times were spent at Drumchapel Elementary School. It was situated across the street from a row of shops, one of which made fresh meat pies. On occasion, if we had the money, some tuppence halfpenny, we would stand by the railing imploring passersby to buy pies for us. In unison we would sing, "We want, what do we want? We want pies!" And sometimes we got lucky.

But it was there that I truly learned to read and write and count. I learned all the tables up to and including the thirteen-times table. I practiced my penmanship and learned to take dictation. Once, when I was away due to illness, I missed the penmanship test. Amazingly, Miss Guy let me take it on my own and gave me a ten out of ten score, thus ensuring I stayed in the back seats. However, my reading still needed work so I had to take home my reading book a few times and practice on my own or with my father.

One day, she told us of a friend who had a baby girl and was trying to decide on a name. They were apparently considering names like Alice or Isabel or Felicia. She then asked the class what they would call a baby. There was a momentary silence during which I blurted out "a nuisance." Much to my embarrassment, the class erupted in laughter.

By this time I was in the highest grade of the three grades taught by Miss Guy. Our classroom was situated between two other classrooms all of which held about 30 pupils. I played football (soccer) using a tennis ball on the playground virtually every day.

Miss Guy also encouraged us to help with the war effort. I went all around the neighbouring houses asking for used magazines and silver paper, which I rolled into a ball. Frank also did his part by serving as a warden for the area. This was important for, armed with a torch, he guided people in dangerous areas. Without torches there was a total blackout.

For a time I went to Sunday school, mainly to join the Life Brigades which operated out of the church. This was an interesting experience at first, especially the hot chocolate we received at the end of a meeting. I got no joy marching all over the church hall.

Once, during an air raid in the middle of the night, the siren blared driving us to our Anderson shelter. My father refused to get out of bed. The sky was filled with search lights. As we huddled there, the sound of bombs and guns were so close it was nerve-racking. At any moment we expected a bomb to explode on top of us. This was exacerbated when my father appeared, hair on end, at the entrance to the shelter in his dressing gown. But it finally went quiet and we returned to our beds. Sometimes we were so exhausted that we slept through the siren and did not learn until the morning that there had been an air raid.

I often explored the land around Drumchapel.

In those days, one was in easy reach of farms and burns (streams) and woods. Once I came across an enormous gateway called the Girnin' Gates, a puzzling place that seemed like a giant door to nowhere. It was set in a wooded area and I recall one autumn, ploughing through a carpet of fallen leaves looking for ancient artifacts, like swords or dirk handles, which I believed were hidden there. I surmised that they were known as "girning" (a Scottish word for whimpering) due to the sound of creaky, rusty gates. Then I heard that it was from two lions, which once adorned the entrance. Like gargoyles, they were so designed that, when it rained, the water would spout from their mouths. But their mouths became clogged and so the water poured from their eyes, like tears.

There was also, what seemed to be, an abandoned brick works nearby, not far from a chicken farm. There were many bricks lying around a half-built structure. I would often think of this place at night. I thought that, if I left home, I could build a small dwelling there. But I wrestled with some difficulties. Where would I find food? I wondered.

Occasionally, Frank would have visitors to the house. During such visits I usually wandered around the backyard or otherwise looked for ways to amuse myself. It was during one such visit, I found a ladder at the back of the house propped up against the sill of the bathroom window. I think Frank had been washing the windows, but whatever the case, the window of the bathroom was wide open. It seemed to me an invitation to test my mettle. So, though it was a little scary, I slowly climbed the steps to the bathroom window. When I reached the top, I lost the confidence to go back down and so I chose the easy way. I simply climbed through the window into the bathroom, then ran downstairs and went back into the garden.

Later, my father asked me if I had climbed the ladder. Afraid that it could spell trouble, I said no, where upon he led me into the bathroom and showed me some very incriminating hand prints, that could only have been made from the outside, and were clearly small-boy size. My father became angry and told me I would be punished, but only after Frank's visitors had left. For the next few days, I worried myself sick in anticipation of the upcoming beating.

Finally, the visitors left, and my mother told me my father wanted to see me in his room. He was in bed, as usual, but he had a long thin bamboo cane in his hand. I could see where it was going and immediately began to tremble in fear. He ordered me to lie across the couch alongside his bed face down. But as I started to do this, he stopped me and told me to pull down my trousers. That was too much. Even as I complied, I began to sob. The humiliation was unbearable. I was gutted like a dead fish. I felt utterly helpless. My self-respect extinguished. My spirit broken. I felt trapped and alone in my fear. As usual, my mother stayed downstairs watching her daughter, and Frank was nowhere to be seen. I felt I was of no consequence. I was nothing.

Distraught, I lay across the couch with my trousers pulled down crying uncontrollably. Wanting to curl up, wanting to disappear, wanting to escape, I waited for the sting of the cane. The inner pain was unbearable.

Suddenly, I was told to pull my trousers up and go. At the last minute, my father seemed to realise that any further punishment would be redundant. It was over. As compensation, I seem to remember he gave me a sixpenny piece. But it was not over. Though my father never again punished me physically in any way, all my confidence was destroyed. I had been molded into a pitiful, diffident being, to be forever haunted by a reoccurring sense of fear and inferiority.

*   *   *

Sometime earlier, in February, I had gone

merrily into town to shop with Irene. I know it was February for I remember bringing back a Valentine's card for my mother. I also recall how I agonized over this purchase, which devoured a large portion of my spending money. But I was taken aback by the indifference with which she received it. Instead of a warm hug, or some such gesture, she simply thanked me and carried on with her work at hand. That was the first time I became aware that my mother did not much care for me, while she was obviously unequivocally devoted to her legitimate daughter, who could do no wrong. Then or later, I realised that she never once attempted to protect me from my father's wrath.

Still, my father did caring things. With wartime rationing of food, we were only allowed one egg per person each week. My father, almost always ate breakfast in bed, and had his egg boiled. But sometimes, he would only eat the top cut off portion of the egg and send the bulk of it to me. Once, when my mother brought me the egg and I began to eat it, I was surprised when it fell in on itself. On this occasion he had eaten the egg and sent in only the top propped up on the empty shell. Of course, I was totally fooled and surprised when the egg collapsed.

Once in a while, my father would call me into his room to play dominoes. He sat up in bed and I sat at the foot. I still have that set of dominoes, which must now be seventy years old.

In the summer of that year, we went to Ayre for a holiday. It was my father's favourite place for it had miles of golden sand along the beach. But instead of a happy-holiday atmosphere, it was a grim reminder that we were a country at war. Huge coils of barbed wire lined the beach as far we could see, walking along the boardwalk. And few people seemed to have gone there for a holiday.

Walking exhausted my father, so my mother got him a wheelchair, which he submitted to very reluctantly. As my mother pushed him along the deserted boardwalk, my father looked beyond the barbwire, but he could not have seen much. For the first time in my life, I saw the eyes of my father, this lion of a man, filled with tears.

That night I had a difficult time sleeping. I had to share a bed with a man I did not know, and I felt uncomfortable. My father slept nearby on the top of a bunk bed, but he was clearly delirious. He spoke constantly in nonsensical sentences. I recalled words like "ticket" and "bus," but more often they did not seem to be words at all. I wished he would stop so I could get some sleep. In fact, after a time, I wished he was dead. This petulant, momentary thought was to haunt me all my life.

* * *

It was the night of 12th of October, 1943, a night I remember well. My mother told me that my father wanted to speak to me before I went to bed. I sensed an air of formality I had not known before, but I went to his bedside as requested. My father was lying on his back with his knees up. He seemed to be very calm and tranquil. I too was calm, for I knew this was not to be a reprimand, and that I was safe. These were the moments I felt my love for him.

He told me that he wanted me to do him a favour. He told me that if anything were to happen to him, I would become the man of the house. He made me promise to look after my mother and sister. Without question, I said that I would. We said goodnight and I kissed him on the cheek, and went to my bed in the nursery. I doubt that I fully understood the import of his words at that time. Never did I think they would be so engraved in my mind.

Sometime, in the early hours of October 13th, my mother woke me to tell me my father was dead. Numbed and sleepy-headed, I followed my mother into the bedroom where my father rested peacefully on his back, his knees still slightly bent. Frank was already in the room. Though dead, he looked exactly like he did when he was alive. In fact, he looked so normal that Frank had to get a mirror, which he held in front of my father's mouth, to see if he was breathing. But it showed nothing.

My mother explained that during the night, she awoke to find it very quiet. She touched my father to see if he was all right, only to feel his cold and lifeless body.

There were no tears. The mantra went though my mind, if it was not reiterated by my mother. "He was better off dead." And so the general feeling was that this was not a bad thing. Death had taken him out of a miserable life. I recall noticing some small yellow pills lying on top of the trolley beside his bed. I knew what they were. I knew they were morphine, and few were left.

My mother made up a makeshift bed in the dining room, where we lay down to try and get more sleep. But my mother sat up, and for the first time in all my life, I saw her light and smoke a cigarette, before I fell asleep.

The following morning, after breakfast, I was dispatched to tell my grandma and Aunt Jean. And after that, I was to go on and tell my Aunt Nan, who also lived in Partick. I was given directions, which I believe I knew already, on taking the bus to Anniesland Cross, then taking a second bus or streetcar down to Partick Street. It was the trip to

Auntie Nan's I had to remember, for we rarely went there.

After I left grandma's house and began my walk to Aunt Nan's, I felt a sense of importance, a sense of purpose. I felt I was emancipated. After all, I had an important mission, and I travelled the streets of Glasgow on my own.

Aunt Nan lived in a flat in a red-bricked tenement complex. I worried a little about finding it in the maze. But I did. My knock on the door was answered by my Uncle Dave. After telling him of my mission, he led me to the kitchen, where Aunt Nan was at the sink, washing up some dishes. Without any to-do, I told her my father was dead, and she immediately slumped over the kitchen sink. She said something to the effect that she knew it would happen, but that it was still a shock. She asked me when it happened, and I told her what little I knew. Then, poste haste, I went home.

The next day, my father's body was placed in a coffin lying on two supports across the front of the fireplace in Frank's bedroom. There was a peculiar smell, which I called the smell of death, but was probably formaldehyde. When I saw my father's body, I was surprised how youthful he appeared. The lines of his forehead seem to have melted away. However, overnight, his jaw sagged and so someone placed a card, not the more usual

Bible, under his chin to hold his mouth together.

Over the next two days, flowers began to arrive, though I understood that he did not want flowers at his funeral. I took them upstairs to place them around my father's coffin. Each time I entered that room, and saw my father's body stretched out before me, I could hardly believe that he was dead. He was so still, but I half-expected him to sit. Also, I recall feeling quite comfortable in that room. My father was no threat to me now. Also, it was so quiet and peaceful there in contrast to the noisy chatter of the people downstairs.

That day, or the next, a minister came to the house. There were several people there, but I hardly saw them and they rarely, if at any time, spoke to me. But when the minister spoke, everyone went silent. Finally, he said let us pray and everyone bowed their head. I cannot recall what he said, but he spoke of my father having gone, no doubt to a better place. It was at that moment I realized the magnitude and finality of my loss. And I broke down and cried. Gone forever was this drummer boy, this romantic heart, this loyal soul, this generous being, this sick and angry man who had lived but half of a half of a life. Gone forever was my father.

I recall, very well, my Uncle Dave placing his hand on my shoulder, and how much that comforted me. Because of that moment, I have always held my Uncle Dave in esteem.

That day they closed my father's coffin and carried it out to the hearse. There was a procession of cars with my mother and I in the lead car behind the hearse. It was a slow procession and I remember wondering how much longer it would take to reach the cemetery.

My father was to be buried in Arkleston Cemetery, Section L, Lair No. 17, in the County of Renfrew. When we arrived, my father's coffin was carried beside the grave site in which the hole had already been dug. There were sashes all around the coffin and I was given the sash at the heard of the coffin. Slowly we lowered it into the hole. I remember little else. My mind was numbed by all the events in the last few days. Somehow we ended up back home, where my father's quiet and empty bedroom seemed unreal to me.

But there was one piece of business yet to be done. We had to go to church on Sunday for a special service commemorating my father. There I had the oddest sensation. While the minister's words went over my head, I stared at him fascinated by his face. I was stunned by the fact that he looked exactly like a picture of a pharaoh I had seen in a book on archeology. And I wondered if reincarnation was a real possibility.

Life at 17 Golf Drive was immediately different with my father gone. As the new "head" of the family, I slept in his place on the bed and so gained control of his Echo wireless. My father had left an envelope in a jacket pocket to be opened in the event of his death. When my mother opened it, she found twenty crisp £1 notes and a piece of paper written on by my father that said: "It is surprising how one can carry on living even when by all the laws one should be in one's grave."

Twelve days later, I "celebrated" my tenth birthday.

Me at about 3

Me at 7, parents, sister

My father (in front) at Ochil Hills Sanatorium

Me and my bike at 16

JACK SMART, in "Fun in a Cabaret," due at Palace Theatre, Newcastle.

My Uncle Jack

The launching of the Queen Mary, 1936

Second Avenue, Clydebank (Note unattended children)

Radnor Street, Clydebank (demolished 1941)

Drumchapel Elementary School and playground

Woodside Senior Secondary School

Woodside School, University of Glasgow at back.
Photo by my Headmaster Mr. McVean.

CHAPTER TWELVE

My tenth birthday was one of the few that stands out in my mind. Though I realised that I would not get the piano lessons I had been promised, I asked for a paint set, not oils mind you, just a plain tin box with little squares of watercolours. It did not happen. Instead, my mother bought me a leather jerkin, which I wore with a measure of pride and a sense of importance. However, when I went to school, I was expected to wear it with a kilt. Like most Scottish boys, I was proud of my heritage but I dreaded the inevitable teasing and jokes that came with this garb. "Only girls wear skirts," and "what are ye wearing underneath?" "Mind yer ain business," never seemed a strong enough response.

It was two or three weeks after my tenth birthday before I realised that being an adult was not an easy thing. My work began at six o' clock in the evening when my mother left to go to her job as a hat-check girl at Plato's restaurant. It was a new experience for her—one that got her out of the house and provided her with some social interaction. She did quite well too, for though the pay was small, her tips were excellent due to the generosity of American soldiers, young men themselves, who no doubt flirted with my attractive thirty-year-old Scottish-Irish mother whose smooth face belied her suffering during the past ten years.

We still lived rent free in the main bedroom, with kitchen privileges, in the semidetached house at 17 Golf Drive. It still held a double bed and a cot, all facing the fireplace, which had an electric fire set up in front. To the right of the bed were two windows overlooking a section of Golf Drive lined with houses on both sides. Just below the windows was the couch which my father had me lie on face down, pants off, for a caning. Beside the bed was a table that held an Echo wireless much used by my father before his death.

Each evening I was confined not just to the house, in which I once roamed freely, but to a bedroom, for my job at that time was to watch my four-year-old sister Janice and see to it that she went to bed at eight o'clock each night. Once she had settled down, I too went to bed. As a ten-year-old this was the most boring time of my life. These evenings were an eternity to me and ended only when my mother came home or I fell asleep. But, given the circumstances, and the promise exacted by my father on his death bed, I had no choice.

My solace was the wireless, which I turned on each night. Since it was a long way from children's hour, I had to listen to adult programmes which I often did not understand. Nevertheless I recall listening to silly shows like "Itma, " most of which I did not get, and serious ones like "The Brains Trust." Once in a while I was pleased with myself for guessing an answer to a question I felt I almost understood. But, more often, it would bore me into an early sleep. That was my entertainment, night after night.

There were, of course, other more dramatic moments. Four-year-old children don't always obey their parents never mind a big brother. Though I used every trick I could think off to get her into bed, once in a while she would not be persuaded. This led to arguments, which led to temper tantrums. During one of these tantrums, she whacked me on the arm with a hairbrush. She never did go to bed.

She kneeled on the couch by the window crying and whimpering for hours. She finally went quiet and must have been close to sleeping when she spotted her mother coming home. As soon as our mother entered the room, she burst into tears sobbing profoundly as she complained about me. Whatever it was, it was my fault.

During this time, I wrote my first poem – a pitiful effort, yet oddly prophetic and still remembered. It went as follows:

> *What is this dreary life of ours?*
> *What are those eerie weary hours?*
> *Where is the joy, the games, the fun?*
> *Where is the laughter? No, there's none.*
>
> *Perhaps I could write; perhaps I could prose.*
> *Perhaps I could sing, nobody knows.*
> *But some day I'm sure the fun will all come*
> *Even if I'm poor, there will always be some.*

But there was fun even then. I loved to go to Drumchaple School for I had friends there: Dorothy Lennox, Camilla Calhoun, David Reid and Gordon Fraser. I often spent an hour after school, which finished at four o'clock, kicking a tennis ball back and forth with David or Gordon, working up a sweat. That usually earned some chastisement from my mother. "Where have you been?" or "you shouldn't sweat like that, you could catch a cold."

Still, without a doubt, my dearest friend was Junior Hope. Though much shorter than me, I was tall even then, we were as close as any brothers could be. We were part of a group of four, which usually ended up occupying the back seats, being shuffled in accord with the results of a weekly test, which included dictation and hand writing. That was a time when we all learned the multiplication tables by rote. Miss Guy had to juggle three classes at the same time, and, as we were the most advanced and bored with the twelve-times table, we were assigned to master the thirteen-times table. That kept us quiet.

She also introduced us to a game that the whole class could play. Someone gave us the first letter of an animal, and the rest had to guess what it was. Junior and I eagerly took to this and began to keep notebooks with lists of animal names. That soon led to searching for more esoteric names to confound the class. I began reading dictionaries and eventually searching out books on zoology in the library, using my mother's library card. It all became quite competitive.

One day, Junior gave me a new animal name, "ham yard." I did not believe him but he said it was the name of a snake that he got from his father. He swore it was real and so I reluctantly added it to my list of snakes. Months later, long after we had parted ways, I discovered that there was indeed a cobra called "hamadryad."

Junior's parents lived in what to me was a mansion. His father was said to be associated with either the diplomatic corps or a trade commission of some sort. I was invited to their house once or twice, one of the occasions being a birthday party for Junior. There were other children there and I remember playing musical chairs, which by cunning delays, I ended up the winner and was presented with a comb. There may have been a message there, for I always had a head of thick unruly hair, and trips to the barber were rare occasions requiring a bus trip to Anniesland.

The camaraderie in that class was truly exceptional. We constantly joked with each other and made up little poems. One, at Camilla's expense, was: *Camilla Calhoun went up in a balloon/And didn't come back to the end of June.* It was a sad day for me when Junior left. But sadder days were yet to come.

*   *   *

One cold Sunday morning, when we were all lying in, an envelope was slipped under the door that was to change our lives yet again. It was a message from Cathy, telling us that we had to leave as she was pregnant and she needed the extra space. The pall in our room was instant. Where would we go? We had no money. We had no possessions. Even the bed we slept in was not ours. All we had were the clothes we wore, pots and pans, and our Echo wireless.

With no one to turn to, my mother was forced to impinge on her mother who now lived with my Aunt Jean in a "but and ben" over a shop on a noisy main road in Partick. My grandmother had been allocated this flat after her longtime home was demolished as a result of the Clydebank Blitz.

The kitchen/ dining room/ living room/ laundry room/ bedroom occupied the larger of the two rooms. The bedroom portion was a recess in the wall, just large enough to fit a bed, while the laundry hung from a pulley over the kitchen table to dry from the ever-hot and burning stove. A masterpiece of construction, the stove was the sole source of heat, and maintained a large kettle of boiling water ready for anything from making tea to washing underwear. The back room, just beyond the toilet, was a bedroom and storage area.

This is where we came to live. I have no recollection of being uncomfortable with this arrangement. I was fond of both my grandma and my aunt for they were kind to me. Moreover, I had a newfound independence, free of the fears of my father, and temporarily, at least freed of the burden of "watching" my sister.

I was eventually enrolled in Partick Elementary School, but had to suffer the humiliation of being "set back" a class. Moreover, I was challenged to a wrestling match with a bully-boy, who seemed to me bigger and stronger. I wrestled with him several times during playtime, and to my surprise held my own. Though thin as a rake, I was very wiry and able to wiggle out of his attempted pins. In the end, he grew tired of it and we became friends of a sort.

The classroom was quite large and filled with rows of boys and girls. I recall on one occasion, when our teacher had temporarily left the room, another loudmouthed bully-boy started causing a disturbance. I stood it as long as I could, and though somewhat fearful, I finally stood up and told him to sit down and shut up. Much to everyone's surprise, he did. Then, to my surprise one of the girls called out "Are you in earnest Ernest," and I shrank back into the anonymity of my seat.

A few days later, when my mother met me from school, she teased me saying I was popular with the girls. When I asked why she thought that, she told me she had heard them talking about me. I could not imagine what anyone could be saying about me. But as my mother passed them by, she heard one of them explain that she had said "Are you in earnest Ernest." Red-faced, I was glad when the subject changed.

One Saturday afternoon, my aunt Jean gave me the money to go to see a Walt Disney picture at a theatre just round the corner. I loved the pictures, especially Disney's cartoon movies. She also asked me to drop off at a "sweetie" shop and get her a quarter pound of chocolate drops. I also loved sweeties especially chocolate ones. As I sat in the stalls watching the movie, I looked at the bag of chocolate drops and realised that there were quite a few there. So, I reasoned that if I ate just one, Aunt Jean would not notice. I looked again and registered the fact that there was still a lot of chocolate drops and so I took another one, two, probably three. Then I noticed that the chocolate was melting. So I ate some more lest they went to waste. When I got home, there were about three or four left in the bag. I expected to be in trouble. But my aunt only laughed.

Just as I was settling into the rhythm of my new life, my mother announced she had found a place for us to live. She only needed to get some money to buy furniture. One of the suggestions that came up was to sell our Echo wireless. I was shocked. I had come to love that wireless like a brother. I was so overwrought that I burst into tears at the very idea. In the end, we kept the wireless but managed to acquire a double bed and some other utility furniture.

Once again, we were on the move.

CHAPTER THIRTEEN

Our new home was a small bedroom with a single window overlooking the miden (dust bins) at the back of the tenement where we had lived before. It was on the top story of an old Edwardian building with two flats on each of the three levels. Once homes for the wealthy, our floor had a large dark hall, two large front rooms and two small back rooms, one of which was ours. There was only space for one double bed and so we all huddled together, staying warm with the help of a rubber hot water bottle. Fortunately, none of us took up much room. I imagine the servants quarters had been upstairs in this area where there were more rooms.

There was a toilet in the hall with a wash hand basin and an unusable bath. There were no towels or paper. You brought your own towel and a piece of newspaper when required. Just beyond the toilet was a huge kitchen with two large windows, tubs and a gas range of some sort. There was also an intriguing row of rusty bells high on a wall, close to the ceiling. No doubt these were originally used to summon maid service. On the other side of the kitchen, close to the ten-foot high ceiling, were several mysterious storage areas.

This was not a happy place, but my mother promised to try and get a bigger room from the landlord, named Carson, whom she knew from our stay there seven years before. And I lived for that day.

The largest room was occupied by my Aunt Mollie. She was married to my father's brother John (Jack). They met on the music hall circuit. She was a dancer and he was part of a comedy team called "Smart and Benson." Uncle Jack played the straight man, Smart. And smart he was. I saw his photo in a newspaper once, dressed up in a tie and tails with a top hat to boot. He won a talent contest and appeared in the movie "The Life and Times of Rabbie Burns." He played the minister at Burns's end. At his theatrical peak he played in the Palace in Newcastle "Fun in a Cabaret" and the prestigious Empire Theatre in Glasgow. But he was fond of the drink and his career went downhill.

Uncle Jack fought in WW 1 and, like the young corporal Hitler himself, was gassed at the front lines. It earned him a discharge but may well have been a contributing factor to his weak lungs, which ultimately contracted tuberculosis. They tried a new technique on him, that of collapsing a lung, but it did not work. I once visited him in a hospital, with my mother. He told me then to tell my father that he would see Old Nick before my father. He was wrong.

My Aunt Mollie got me a free ticket to see him in the Empress Theatre on St. Georges Road, which was around the corner from where we lived. I was truly thrilled and the memory of it still burns in my mind. I remember him in a skit where, as usual, he was the smart one with a butler on call. Unfortunately, the butler had a bad stutter which made him difficult to understand. So my uncle told him to stop trying so hard to speak and urged him to sing his words instead, which immediately brought about a vast improvement. A few minutes after the butler left the stage, he came running back stuttering even worse that usual. My uncle told him to slow down, relax, just take a deep breath and sing what he wanted to say. After some hesitation, he sang with an accompanying dance: *The house is on fire, hooray, hooray*. With the audience howling, they both rushed off the stage into a cloud of smoke.

I last saw my Uncle Jack, in bed in a small room connected to Aunt Mollie's large room at Windsor Terrace. I can't remember what he said, but I remember him lying on his right side coughing heavily, and I knew that cough from before.

One day my mother had a friend come to visit. And they talked and talked until it was too late for the woman to go home. To accommodate her, I went to the bottom of our only bed to sleep, which I remember was not very comfortable, and I recall feeling some resentment too. But I always managed to sleep.

Freed temporarily from going to school, I roamed the silent streets around our new home. Directly across from our close (long entrance to a tenement) was Clarendon Street. For reasons I never understood, there was a row of posts running across the street with large spaces between them, which blocked all traffic, except bikes. These presented a challenge I took up. Overcoming some trepidation, I learned to vault over them. But most of the time I loitered alone in the close, out of the rain, just dreaming.

A few months later, my mother was finally able to rent the big room across the hall and soon after she got a separate single bed for me. It was a joyous moment—to have one's own bed in a large bright room. It was one of the happy moments in the tenth year of my life.

It was a remarkable room, two large windows captured all the light available from the outside, and the single light hanging from the centre of the room gave us light when it was dark outside. But summer was approaching, and the short dull days of winter gave way to the long bright days of June and July.

There was a fireplace directly across from the two beds. It was a coal fireplace with a wide hearth and a long marble mantlepiece adorned with a wooden mantle clock. This was an important item for we had no watches and the wireless was not a consistently reliable source of the time. The wireless sat on a small table on the right side of the fireplace beside a wooden armchair. On the other side of the fireplace was another slightly more comfortable chair. A pouffe filled the space between the chairs. Against the wall across from the windows, we had a sideboard in the centre and a wardrobe at the side of that, while just behind the comfortable chair was our kitchen table graced with two square-backed chairs. And behind that, not far from the fireplace was a small gas stove, which we lit with a flint. Finally, tucked away in the corner nearest the table was the press (pantry), which held what food we had, usually only potatoes, flour and sugar. This furniture did not all appear at once but was acquired, from secondhand stores, other people's castoffs and the like, over the ensuing months.

One of the many interesting features of this room was the door panel. It had been hand painted in oil depicting soft pastoral scenes. And so there were flowers, birds, butterflies and bees aplenty. At least there were. Someone painted over them. Untouched, however, were the cornices and the ornate plaster around the ceiling. Lying in bed, I would stare long and hard at these decorations and try to imagine who lived in the house when it was in its prime. By contrast the floor was covered in everyday linoleum, supporting a rug here and there.

This would be my new home for the next eight and a half years, providing me with an element of stability, I had not previously known. I had a warm fire, my own bed and my beloved Echo wireless. It seemed that it had everything I could possibly need.

My mother seemed happy too. She would talk for hours with Aunt Mollie who had a yelpy little Scottish Terrier. Its claim to fame was that on command it would give the Hitler salute. Aunt Mollie had been a dancer but injured her leg that left her with a limp. She also played the banjo-ukelele.

We continued to go to grandma's house for a visit and she always had the kettle ready to boil water for tea One day we learned that she had a stroke, which left her paralyzed down one side. Thereafter, she was confined to bed. She also became more lighthearted, laughing readily at my tomfoolery. But a few months later she died. She was laid out in her bedroom. I saw her body and I was frightened by it. She looked ghastly and I recall her eyes were black and sunken, which scared me and left me unnerved.

During the ensuing months when all the children were on their summer holidays, I came to know and befriend many of them. I was always happiest to have one true male friend, so when I met Bobbie Campbell, and he took a liking to me, we became fast friends. There was also my old girl friend, Janis, with whom I played in the tar and I fell in love with her all over again. Amazingly, she still lived in the same flat, but she had grown to be taller than me at that point, which I found inhibiting.

Sometimes my Aunt Mollie would ask me to carry her banjo-ukelele to the band stand in some park. She performed in these with a friend who sang, after which my aunt would perform solo on the instrument. Of course, she would give me a couple of bob. I thought she was great.

Soon the summer rolled by, and I had to go back to school. This time it was Napiershall Primary School, my sixth and last elementary school. Still a year behind, I found the work rather easy. Gaining acceptance was harder. Once again I was challenged to fight. This time with a shorter, but much more pugnacious opponent. We fought over several play times, and while nothing was really resolved, I grew to dread this playtime ritual. Finally, I decided I would not be taunted any more, and found a couple of "thrup'ny bits," (three-penny brass coins), which I clenched in my fists to make my punches harder. I kept shooting out my long skinny left arm to keep my opponent at bay. It worked well, but he surprised me by throwing in the towel claiming he could not get near me and that was not fair. We never fought again. Since there were no other challengers, my school days became calm, and for the most part, enjoyable.

One day, during the Easter holidays, my mother told me Uncle Jack had died. Perhaps from my father's death the year before, I was numb to any emotion. A day or two later, I was chatting with the girls on my street. Later, I went to Ruth

Hall's flat where she and Anne and Leslie Smith were playing and knocked on the door to get them to come out. When they opened the door, I learned that they were in the middle of a birthday party, and after some cajoling on my part, I was invited to join them. They seemed to like me and I was excited at joining the party, but I had to first tell my mother where I was. When I ran back home to tell my mother, she stopped me cold. I could not go to a birthday party with my uncle lying dead. So I sulked alone in the close.

The following day, when my uncle was to be buried, and I was loitering in the stair well as usual, my Aunt Esther showed up. As she was about to climb the stairs, she pressed a pound note in my hand. But I recoiled and refused it, telling her grandly that we didn't need any money. I would never see her again.

On June 6th, an army of 155,000 Allied troops crossed the English Channel to land in Normandy. This time they were well prepared, and despite fierce resistance from the Germans, they fought their way into France marking what was known as D-Day. It was the largest amphibious military operation in history, and the beginning of the end of the German Third Reich.

On September 3, exactly four years after Britain's declaration of war on Germany, the Allied

122

Forces liberated Brussels. The Germans, however, were far from finished. They hurled V1 and later V2 rockets at London, which caused great devastation. These flying, silent killer bombs could be launched at any time of the day or night, making it difficult to sound the alarm.

In September, my sister, soon to be five years old, began her elementary schooling at Napiershall School. I would be her escort for the year to come.

That winter we developed the routine of going to the pictures every Saturday night at the Seamore picture hall and then rushing home to bed to listen to "Saturday Night Theatre" on the wireless. Often I would bait my sister to race with me to the next lamppost, offering her a start and so on. Something of a teaser, I would let her stay ahead until the last minute, and then just manage to pass her. Still, it left her with the feeling that she might have beat me and she seemed content with that. This was about the only time we fully functioned together as a family.

CHAPTER FOURTEEN

Because I was performing well but was still a class back in my schooling, I was given an opportunity to jump ahead and set my "qualifying exam." This exam determined which secondary school you would be going to. Unfortunately I did not quite score high enough to get to Woodside Senior Secondary School. The alternative was to go on to a trade school, but no one recommended that.

An analysis of my exam papers showed that I had done well in English but fell short in arithmatic. While I could add, subtract and multiply numbers with ease, I had no idea how to deal with fractions. Adding 5/8 to 1/3 was beyond me. My mother was informed of the situation and arrangements were made for me to stay after school to study fractions, not an exciting prospect for an eleven-year-old. Moreover, the headmaster himself undertook the task, which placed me under even greater pressure. Qualifying exams aside, that year I did so well in the exams for my own class that I won the prize for First Boy. For this I was called up to a stage and presented with a book: *The Shakespeare Story Book*, which reduced Shakespeare's plays to simple narrative accounts. I found the stories, in plain English, surprisingly enjoyable.

About this time I decided to maintain a diary, in which I wrote down my personal feelings and the names of girls that I fancied. I kept it in my school bag which lay at my feet when I sat in class. Somehow a sneaky boy behind me got hold of it, causing me tremendous embarrassment. I fought to get it back, and when I did, I destroyed it determined never to maintain a diary again.

That year I was able to get a book from the library, filled with pictures or paintings of tall ships, mostly galleons. I liked them so much I wished I was able to draw them. But I did not feel I had the skill. Instead, I used some tracing paper to draw an outline and then transferred the picture to a drawing tablet. The effect was amazing to me. One day I took my drawing pad to school to show some classmates, only to be met with suspicion. They asked me if I drew them and I said yes. When pressed I admitted that I had used tracing paper. My drawings were immediately met with derision. I was nothing but a copycat, I was told. While I felt that in a way I had drawn them, their comments hurt me. I soon came to think what they said was true. I got rid of the drawings and never tried that again. The thought almost made my skin crawl.

There was a time when my skin did crawl. This was diagnosed as scabies, a nasty little mite that loves living on human flesh. With this I had to suffer the indignity of showering once a week with a medicated soap. These showers were open like prison stalls and shared with others. On one occasion I had a woman next to me scrubbing herself. Though she turned her back to me, I still caught a glimpse of her ample breasts which left me agog. I was too young for lewd thoughts.

I did not know at the time that Hitler, and his loyal servant Goering, had committed suicide. I did know that Germany had surrendered unconditionally to the Allies. That was a joyous day for the British, which they trumpeted as VE-Day. Newsreels showed people dancing in the streets. I was looking forward to the lights being turned on again after almost five years of blackout. I was particularly interested in the lights that framed the

Empress Theatre just around the corner.

While it was a good year for me, and the British people, it was a black day for the people of the world. The Americans, under the leadership of President Harry Truman, chose to drop an atomic bomb on the Japanese people of Hiroshima. And so, on August 6, 1945, 200,000 people—men, women and children—died in the most horrendous individual attack ever perpetrated by one country against another. Not satisfied with that, three days later, they dropped a second atomic bomb on Nagasaki killing another 200,000 people. The Japanese people, who clearly saw the message, finally got their act together and surrendered on September 2, 1945. This day was celebrated as VJ-day, Victory over Japan. It was shock and awe of the highest order. Even many Americans were appalled.

But, in their defense the generous Americans, supported and applauded the subsequent actions of General Douglas MacArthur in leading the reconstruction of that devastated country.

It is possible that these events so shocked Einstein, whose science paved the way for this doomsday weapon, that his hair went gray, curled and grew straight out of his head. There is no question that he would never have condoned such action. Like most thinking people, he knew the power of the atomic bomb could have been demonstrated to Japan without wholesale slaughter. Moreover, the Americans had opened a Pandora's Box.

* * *

It was around this time I began to earn money.

In a small dark and dingy room across the hall from us, lived an old Irish couple, the Keoghs. The man left for work early in the morning and returned late so I rarely saw him. Mrs. Keogh stayed at home with her cat. Her white hair in a bun, her jowls sagging, her back bent over. She was a sad figure to behold. A frail woman, she lay in bed most of the time often gasping for air as she suffered terribly from asthma. I came home one time and found her sprawled half way up the third flight of steps. I took her boney arm, and helped her reach the landing in front of the door, for which she was thankful.

Despite all her troubles, her abject poverty, her fights with her husband, she was a kindly and knowledgeable individual. She read several daily papers cover to cover—she had no wireless—and was fully aware what was going on in the world.

My business relationship came about when I was asked to empty her cat's box, about once per week. It was three flights of stairs and then a walk through the backyard to get to the midden, a daunting task for her. For this service she paid me a sixpence, and so I became a wage earner.

Only later did I realise she was an alcoholic. Once, she was so desperate for a drink, but too weak to go out, she asked me to get her a half-bottle of Scotch. She gave me the money, and the directions to a pub. There, I knocked on a side door, explained the situation, and was slipped the necessary alcohol. For that, she gave me a shilling.

One day, on my way home from a walk in the park, I came across crowds of people lining Great Western Road. I worked my way to the front just in time to see a cavalcade of motors slowly going by. And there he was. Winston Churchill himself. He stood in an open car, showing his two-finger victory sign as people cheered.

But mostly, I spent my time playing the streets or the backyards of the tenements. One favourite game was king's ball, a variation of dodge-em-ball. It started by someone holding a tennis ball between the knuckles of their hands and throwing it to the player next to them. If they caught it, they threw it to the next person and so on. The first person who failed to catch the ball, or drop it, became "it." Then they had to try and hit all of the other players with the ball, knocking them out of the game one by one. Last man standing was the winner. If no one was left, the ball thrower was the winner.

Another game was called "release." This was a weird game where people became "prisoners" in a proscribed area and could only be released by another player running through that area. However, if they were hit by the ball-holder, they too became prisoners. A good ball player could end up having everyone imprisoned, but that rarely happened.

I did not, however, neglect my schooling. One day I, and some others, was asked to enter an inter-school competition by writing an essay on the poetry of Robert Burns. We had studied some of his poems during our regular class time, and I even learned some parts of them by heart. I think it had to be about 500 words, or two or three foolscap pages long. To fill the pages, I peppered them with quotes from the poetry I had memorized. As soon as I had completed my essay, I raced home.

During this time my mother got by with a widow's pension, and some odd jobs as a cleaning lady for a wealthy, or at least, wealthier, relative of the Moores. She occasionally came home with a jacket or some other piece of clothing no longer wanted by her employers. Fortunately, they were about the same size and I suspect, they were not too far apart in age.

At Xmas, my sister and I always shouted up the lum (chimney) with me first as I was trained to say: "Anything you like. Thank you." I had stopped believing in Santa Claus, years before. Next morning we were always surprised by Santa's gifts. I typically received a Dandy or Beano Album, a net-like stocking stuffed with miscellaneous items such as a tin whistle, as well as a sock holding an orange. It was never quite what I wanted, such as a chemistry set. But I was content enough.

CHAPTER FIFTEEN

Early in the year, 1946, I was surprised to be awarded with a Certificate of Merit for Distinction in Scottish Literature from the Burns Federation. It seems they were impressed by my extensive use of quotes from Burn's poetry. I still remember my teacher, as he gave the news, looking at me quizzically. *Who is this boy anyway?*

During my last days at Napiershall School, I became friends with a boy called Hamilton Dunning, and another called Gerald Buchan with the nickname of Bucky. Gerald was an easygoing boy, who liked to hang around with me. He had not rid himself of the habit of sticking two fingers into his mouth under his front teeth, which may have accounted for his nickname. Our teacher, Mr. McIsaac tried to shame him out of it. For a time it seemed to work, but then, as his concentration faded, his hand would move unconsciously back to his mouth. Once Mr. McIsaac made him sit facing the wall at a corner of the classroom, cruelly referring to him as a dunce. This was too much for Bucky and he broke into tears, which for some reason raised my ire, though I said nothing. I think I expressed some understanding to Gerald, which was enough to make him a loyal friend.

Mr. McIsaac did some strange things. Once, to fill time, he had us play a kissing game, whereby someone would stand behind the large blackboard on wheels, and tell him the name of the boy or girl he or she wanted to kiss. He then called on the person to go around the backboard to be kissed. Fortunately, it was a big class, and he did not have enough time to get around to me. Another time he had all the boys line up in front of the classroom, and tell the class what his father did for a living. As it moved along the line closer and closer to me, I felt a rising panic. When he finally asked me what my father did, I broke into tears croaking that my father was dead.

Hamilton Dunning was a bright kid, more like my old pal Junior Hope. We seemed able to relate to each other in a way we were not always able to relate to others and that was enough for our bond of friendship.

There was another boy in my class, a rowdy but seemingly an easy-going boy called Louis, which we pronounced Looey. He was involved in a few scraps but none involved me. Oddly, although it was a mixed class, I cannot recall the name of a single girl. The girls I knew from my street were more upper middle class and went to Hillhead.

One day, coming home from school, there was a man with a wheel barrow on the street yelling: "Money for rags." What an opportunity I thought. I rushed upstairs to tell my mother who produced a small bundle of unusable clothing. I think I got a sixpence. On another occasion, I got a plate dish. After that, I ignored him.

Soon it was again time to set my qualifying examinations. With my First Boy award, my Certificate of Merit and special tuition in fractions, I was considered a shoo-in for Woodside School. Aside from the time we took writing the examinations, we seemed to have lots of free unstructured time. Now a senior elementary school pupil, I was charged with checking on the furnace and so had access to a room others did not have. I was often there with Hamilton and Bucky. We talked excitedly about what we were going to do in life. Our plan then was to travel to south America and sail down the Amazon river. To us, action and adventure were the stuff of life.

I went down there, with Hamilton Dunning and Bucky, right after our exam. We talked about the exam, recalling questions and comparing our answers. While most of our answers were in accord, occasionally we had answers that were different and one or two of us would realise that we were wrong. In due course Bucky went home and Hamilton and I returned to our classroom for a pencil or something. The room was absolutely empty, no kids, no teachers, no one. However, we noticed a stack of files lying on the teacher's desk, which turned out to hold the exam papers we had handed in earlier. Mindful of at least one wrong answer he had made, Hamilton pulled out his paper and changed it. I was appalled but did nothing about it.

A few weeks later we got the results of our qualifying exam. These results determined which school one went to. My friend Bucky was put down for Garscube Road School, which was designed to train you for one of the trades, plumbing, etc. I was set to go to Woodside Senior Secondary School, which was academically oriented and the pathway to Glasgow University, whose very name caused me excitement. I was shocked to learn that

Hamilton Dunning was going to Alan Glen High School, a private school for the wealthy. This school offered a scholarship to a few pupils with the highest test results from the public elementary schools. Hamilton's score exceeded mine by a single point.

*　*　*

The summer of 1946 saw me playing in the streets as before. Tommy McCarthy was an older boy who lived in the same tenement as Bobby, just across the way. He liked to play too, but he played rough and bordered on being a bully-boy. He claimed that he liked to catch flies and screw off the heads to see how they flew headless. Once we had a battle where he took on both Bobby and me. It began in fun with us throwing clods at each other, ripping up tufts of grass to get them. Then it deteriorated into throwing stones. At this point each side took refuge in a back stairwell, which acted like a bunker. And it was just as well. Tommy, a big and very strong lad, threw his stones, with such ferocity that he could have killed us. Fortunately, we always ducked in time.

On another occasion, he chased after us with a pellet gun and shot me in the back of the neck as I ran. He immediately apologized, but it stung. On yet another occasion I watched a backyard cricket match that boiled down to Jackie versus Tommy contest. Jackie was about the same age as Tommy, sixteen I would guess, and lived with his parents in a flat just above Anne and Leslie. Tommy began ripping the ball at Jackie until he gave up.

Years later, he joined the Merchant Navy and once, on a visit home, he stopped by Sam's Pool Hall and seeing us poaching in the dark, he gave Sam the money to turn on the lights so we could play legitimately. Jackie grew up to be a barber.

Once I had an occasion to walk through a nearby neighbourhood with which I was not very familiar. There were kids on the street, but I paid them no mind. That is, not until they swarmed around me demanding to know what I was doing there. The situation became very tense and threatening. My reasons were somewhat lame and I could see I was in deep trouble. As they inched in on me, they said this is Louis's territory—you don't belong here. That was my opening. I told them I was a good friend of Louis and that we had been in the same class in school, which was true. I also told them that, I just talked to him a week or two ago at the furniture shop where he worked. This was not all true for though I had seen him, we never talked. But my claim was enough to convince them to back off and let me through. I was pretty relieved.

It was about this time, after much pestering, I got a second-hand bike—a 26-inch policemen's bike. No gears, no lights, nothing fancy, but I loved it. I cycled all over the place, roads, backyards, pavements. Before long, I could stand up on the saddle, which had no springs, and cycle backwards by placing one leg under the cross bar. My balance was so honed I could literally turn the bike around while staying on the same spot.

However, on one occasion I was racing down a hill when the bracket holding the front mudguard broke spinning it around in a flash to lock my front wheel. It was so abrupt that I was literally thrown from the bike, somersaulted in the air and crashed to the ground on my back. Amazingly, apart from shock and abrasions, I was not seriously hurt. On another occasion I deliberately flirted with death, riding full speed through an intersection without checking for cars.

One summer day, Bobby and I cycled out to the Bluebell Woods. This was several miles away at the end of a tramline. Bobby's tire got ripped so he could no longer cycle—a tricky situation. Finally we decided that he would take the streetcar home and I would cycle back holding his bike beside mine with one hand. That was tricky, but my energy level was so high at the time that I not only returned safely nonstop, but kept up with the streetcar, which, by stopping now and then, gave me the time to catch up when I slipped behind.

We also discovered a locked cupboard in the bottom floor of the tenement across from mine. It was so large, I decided that I could use it as my personal laboratory. I was long interested in chemistry and had compiled a list of secret formulae and other chemical information, such as the periodic table of elements, which I kept in three large notebooks. We found a padlock to secure the door. We had no key, but Bobby was skilled at opening padlocks with the sharp end of a broken dart—a skill he shared with me.

With my lab secured, I brought in my note books and other paraphernalia including a supply of candles and matches. A week or two later, I returned to find my lock gone and the door ajar. When I found that all my books were gone, I was shattered. I could not believe that someone from some other area would break into my lab and be so mean-minded as to steal my work.

During one of our trips to the countryside we came across a pond surrounded by baby frogs. The urge to catch them was irresistible. We rounded up perhaps 15 to 20 of these little creatures. Not knowing quite what to do with them, I decided this would be an opportunity to populate our barren backyards with wild life. So we brought them home and released them into the backyards between Windsor Terrace and Glenfarg Street. Concerned about their food supply (I think we thought they ate greens) we went far and wide pulling up clods of grass and replanting them in the area we had released the frogs. With our mission complete, we were chased off by a downpour in the comforting knowledge that the frogs would feel quite at home in the rain. Two or three weeks later, we could not find any of the frogs and were never sure if they had travelled to greener pastures or become a source of food for the crows and the cats.

On a trip by bus to the botanical gardens we marvelled at the variety of plants and the hot climate they endured. We searched for and found some banana trees but, yes, they had no bananas. We did find some heavily laden tomato plants and, driven by thirst from the heat, and the fact that no one was around, we plucked a few for personal consumption. Bobby ate his more or less on the spot, while I harboured mine in a pocket of my jacket until we were safely on the bus back home. They were so sweet and delicious, I remember them to this day.

One of my favourite holiday resorts was Dunoon with it sandy beaches and clean salty air. It was a short trip from Glasgow to Gourock, and in the ferry from there to Dunoon. Though less than an hour away, it was a completely different world from the streets of Glasgow. It was along its beaches that I spent most of my time, searching the waters edge for who knows what treasures that may have been washed up by the tide. Inevitably, I was loaded down with shells and stones and anything else that looked interesting. Once, I cornered a small crab and was so taken by it, I brought it home. Unfortunately, when I opened the tin, where I kept it, the crab jumped out and escaped into our dark hall. And, I could not find it. Days later it turned up under a door, dead as a doornail.

With the summer holidays over, I now faced the challenge of high school and I had no idea what to expect. Moreover, I was about to become a teenager though I had no idea what that meant either.

A couple of weeks before that birthday, the last of the NAZI bigwigs, Herman Goering, committed suicide. But just as the NAZI era was coming to a close, the "cold" war with the Soviet Union was beginning. As Winston Churchill put it, "An iron curtain has descended across the Continent."

We had our own cold war. During the winter the coalman would work his way along Windsor Terrace delivering coal. The coal was piled in sacks on top of a large flat cart pulled by a powerful Clydesdale horse. These horses, bred in Scotland were exceptionally strong. Now used primarily for show, there once were 140,000 such horses working in Scotland.

When he came to our close, he put his hand to the side of his mouth and, in a loud but musical tone, called: "coooooooooal" His voice resinated all the way up the stairs alerted everyone that he was there. If I was sent down with the money, he would go to his cart, swing a bag of coal onto his shoulders, which were protected by a leather cover, and trudge up the stairs dumping the coal into our box in a small cupboard off the hall.

One week it turned very cold after a rainfall making the street treacherously slippery. We badly needed coal to heat our room, but the coalman refused to bring his Clydesdale into the terrace. My only option was to drag the sack of coal along the street, and up the stairs, one at a time. I did it, but it left me drained and in admiration of the strength of our coalman.

CHAPTER SIXTEEN

I was excited about going to Woodside School. It opened up the door to many things, things I never even dreamt of. Though the school taught both boys and girls, they were placed in different classes. Only later, in the fourth and fifth years were the classes blended, My first class was MB. Since we never understood what that was meant to signify, we called ourselves the Mad Boys. We were also allocated to one of the schools four houses, which in my case was Kelvin.

All the tuition was divided into periods. We had periods for English, French, Mathematics, Science, Art, Geography and History. In addition we had a period for PT (physical training) and every morning we came together for twenty minutes in the Home room for general information and Bible study. No one did much Bible studying, and it soon became a time to catch up on homework or just laze around. There were toilet breaks for nature calls, or a quick smoke at the back of the toilet room, which was located outside the school. The teachers used the staff room. One could literally see the smoke pouring out from the bottom of the door.

Though there were only seven subjects, many of them were subdivided. Maths, for example, could be arithmetic, algebra, geometry, trigonometry and so on. Then there was the burden of homework, especially weekend homework, which always included writing an essay, reading specified chapters of a book or memorizing a poem or other material.

For 2/6 (half-a-crown), you could join the school club which proffered an array of activities every day of the week. Yet, despite all the choices, I could not bring myself to join. Most involved expenditures I could not afford. One could hardly join the camera club without a camera. But it was more than that. I had to wrestle with a growing diffidence.

Eventually, I surprised even myself, by joining the Highland Light Infantry Cadets. They called it the Army Cadet Unit. I cannot recall the attraction—it may have been the khaki army uniform, which you got for joining. This was the real thing, complete with a greatcoat, gaiters, belt and cap. We met after school one day per week and paraded about the central hall, and sometimes, out in the playground. We practiced standing at attention and at ease and we marched and marched wheeling about left and right. This was not particularly exciting or different from the Life Boys, but we spent the occasional weekend in an army barracks. There we were issued old, heavy WW 1 rifles. We marched with these, learnt to present arms and other soldierly things. We were also expected to run 100 yards in 13 seconds with full gear. Not everyone could do this. Once we went on a trip in a "duck." This was a motorised transport vehicle that ran on land and water, after an adjustment. I enjoyed these weekends, except that we were awakened at five in the morning by a bagpiper marching through the dormitories. However, after making our bed (arranging the biscuits) and passing inspection, we happily marched to the cafeteria hungry for a full breakfast. At the end of a year, promotions were made. I had expected to be promoted to lance-corporal, but was passed over. I lost interest after that and left.

Still, during that first year of high school, I found that I was quite good at everything academic. I was at, or near the top of my class on every subject. After the first year's final exams, I placed third overall in my class.

Unfortunately, I may have been at the bottom of my class in hygiene. While I signed (washed) my face every morning using a small basin of warm water, the rest of my body was neglected. I made this amazing discovery when I scratched my groin and saw the skin scraping off leaving white patches. After that, when my mother and sister were out, I put our large round tub-like basin in front of the fireplace, poured in some boiling water, adding cold water as needed, and bathed.

My teeth were another problem. My mother, my grandma and my Aunt Jean all had false teeth. My teeth, of course, were real, though an unreal green colour. My aunt fixed this by holding me in a headlock and rubbing my teeth with a cloth soaked in bleach. I did have a tooth brush, but we rarely had any toothpaste. When we did, it was a hard paste in a small round tin. At someone's suggestion, I tried brushing my teeth with soot garnered from the chimney. I soon abandoned that idea preferring to simply rub my teeth with my finger—not very hygienic as my nails were rarely cut and were edged with a dark substance generally referred to as "durt."

Then there was my hair. Here I was most

fortunate, for my mother washed it several times a year. But it was not always enough, for I got head lice (boosies we called the little creatures) and for a time I enjoyed combing them onto a paper and squishing them. They were finally extinguished by the application of some scalp-burning chemical.

Every morning I combed my hair, wetting the comb under the tap in the kitchen, which was directly in front of the window. These windows opened and there was one time, when I was quite fed up, that I opened one and sat on the sill contemplating suicide by jumping. I have forgotten the actual time, and the reason. Fortunately, the feeling passed.

That summer, the first Edinburgh International Festival and Fringe festival opened, while in Glasgow almost every park had a band shell providing a stage for entertainment of all kinds. We were fortunate enough to live close to a large park called Kelvin Grove Park. It boasted a putting green, tennis courts and a large busy duck pond. At the far end of the park stood the Glasgow Art Gallery and Museum. Often, on a Sunday, I would take the long walk there and marvel at the stuffed animals, the racks of insects, the artifacts from different cultures. It had many rooms and took some time to get around. It would have taken all day if you chose to gaze at all the paintings, many by the old masters and many so filled with soldiers, horses, castles that it took several paces to go from one end of the painting to the other. When I did look, it was usually at the many plump nudes. Sundays were tranquil days. But other days could be rough.

I did not like John Cuthbertson. A wiry boy about my age and height, he lived among the foulmouthed Garscube Road area boys and I felt that he had no business on Glenfarg Street. Moreover, I was raised to believe that the use of bad language was a reflection of the paucity of your vocabulary or in a word, ignorance.

We met by accident outside the clinic. I asked him why he was there and suggested that he go back to his own place. But he was belligerent and not about to move. So we started to argue and then push each other. Before long it was a full-scale bare-knuckled fight, the likes of which I had never known. Time and time again he hurt me with his heavy-handed punches to my head and face. Time and time again I hurt my knuckles hammering his head. But I was not going to yield. It was my turf. We swung at each other nonstop with lefts and rights. Neither of us tried to defend ourselves, we were too busy punching. We just slugged it out, punch after punch after punch. Somehow we collided and fell to the ground outside the clinic.

There we wrestled, pulling, pushing rolling over each other blissfully unaware of anyone who may have seen us. We were sweating now. Our hair was askew. Our clothes were in disarray. Still, quitting was not an option. Then suddenly it was over. Someone appeared from nowhere and emptied a bucket of cold water over us. Soaked to the skin, and ordered to break it up, we silently wandered off in different directions. I never saw him again, nor did I ever fight again.

*   *   *

In September, the start of my second year at high school, my class was called 2F. We did not know what to make of that either. It was not like there was a 2E.

In October of that year I reached the awkward age of fourteen. That year also, I got my first real job working for a grocer. For ten bob (shillings) a week I delivered boxes of groceries to people all around the neighbourhood. It was back breaking work, for I had neither a delivery bike nor barrow. Sometimes I had to lug boxes great distances. Moreover, I often had to climb two or three flights of stairs. Occasionally, I was tipped with a thrupence (a silver threepenny bit) or sixpence. The customers were often old people who could probably barely afford the groceries in the first place.

The manager often kept me waiting in the back store room—once I got so hungry I ate a couple of tea cakes from his inventory—every Friday I received ten shillings, which I turned over to my mother. She, in turn, would give me half-a-crown as pocket money. It was wonderful for a fourteen-year-old to have a couple of shillings in his pocket. That could get me into two picture shows and buy me a five-pack of Woodbine cigarettes.

This went well for many weeks, until on one of these deliveries, I was stopped short by a sharp pain in my left lung. It seemed like a knife had been stuck in my chest, This became an ongoing problem for most of my life. Many years later, it was to be diagnosed as a pneumothorax, where a small pocket of air escapes from the lung then presses against the outer wall. There was never a thought of seeing a doctor in those days. I just worked through it.

Still with energy to burn, my friend Bobby and I would shinny up drain pipes, climb over walls, explore abandoned buildings, usually "dunnys" that had become too unhealthy for people to live. In Australia, a dunny is a cesspool. Each night after tea, usually the last meal of the day, I would hear three knocks on the wall beside our front door and know it was Bobby. We would then take off into the night (in winter it was dark just after 4 p.m.) to see what challenge we could find. Usually we tested ourselves by climbing over walls or scaling buildings to reach their roof. We formed our own club which included an identifying badge. I suppose this was in case we did not recognize each other in the dark. We also had a motto: Valour is Greedy of Danger, VIGOD for short. Not original but which, I at least thought, was appropriate. I enjoyed playing the detective even when there was no crime to solve. We took careful note of the discarded cigarette packages, and indeed started to collect them, pounding the street, rifling though rubbish boxes. I also kept a notebook of all the tricks criminals could use, which in truth I learned from the pictures. The only one I recall now was the trick of wearing your shoes backwards when you walked across a garden to break into a house. This, I thought, could be used to fool the police into thinking they were the footprints of someone who *left* the property.

We loved to explore and kept an open eye for abandoned houses and the like. We found one on my side of Windsor Terrace just before St. George's Road. It was a boarded up basement flat and the door was locked. However, that was no deterrent to us. We got through the door and soon established it as our own. We overcame the scary darkness with lit candles, which also helped dampen the musty smell. Exploring it room by room, we found nothing but strange markings on some of the walls and the skeletal remains of a cat. But we had a place of our own which, on account of the markings, I dubbed the Magic House. Our plan was to make it the base of our yet to materialise secret society. But we were so secret there was never any society.

Once, on a dare by Bobby, I went into the Magic House alone and without light. As proof I had to make a mark on the most distant wall so Bobby could see I got there. Eventually, someone found out that the door was breached and it was re-boarded more tightly than ever.

Occasionally, we had played a game of throwing a stone or a coin towards a wall, to see who could get closest. We also used milk tops for this. These were round pieces of cardboard on top of a full bottle of milk. And it just so happened that around the corner was a milk factory. So one dark night, we "cased" the property to find a way in and we did. Moreover, we found a storage area with scores and scores of brand-new milk tops. We did not think they would miss a few dozen or so.

Around this time my mother got a job as an usherette at a picture theatre. I liked that job, for on occasion, she would slip me in to see a picture without paying. On the other hand I was back "watching" my little sister and that would keep me in at night. Once, however, I was having such a good time playing outside with some kids, I rebelled at my confinement. So, after my mother had left for work, and Janice had gone to sleep, I slipped outside to resume playing. Janice was about eight years old, while I would be fourteen.

CHAPTER SEVENTEEN

Like many, I was shocked to learn of the assassination of Mahatma Gandhi. I saw it on a newsreel at the cinema. I was amazed to see this small defenseless man shot at point blank range.

About this time my mother landed a job at a school cafeteria. This was a godsend for us, for she was able to bring home some of the leftovers to help fill our empty stomachs. However, it meant she was away from home during the midday dinner (lunch hour). Actually, we got an hour and a half. It, therefore, fell upon me to make dinner each day for myself and my sister. Mostly I was frying sausages or black pudding with sliced potatoes. There was always some sort of desert, if only a tangerine.

We especially looked forward to Tuesdays. That day, my mother left us the Dandy or the Beano to read. They alternated with each other every week. My sister, now about nine years old, wanted it as much as I did and would rush to get home first to grab the comic, not to mention the biggest or choicest piece of cake or whatever was left for us. This led me into running home from my school, a far greater distance. I usually won, but not always. Inevitably there were squabbles over this and the food and complaints filed with my mother when we got home from school. However, by that time I had usually lost interest and wanted to listen to the Children's Hour on the wireless.

I continued to do quite well in school. One day, when Mr. Lochie, our music teacher, was handing out our marks, he asked me to stand up. I remember he stared at me for some time during which my knees almost buckled. I think he mumbled something about me being glaikit enough. Finally, he told me that I had the highest mark—an unheard off 90 percent. Needless to say I was proud of that. Music was always one of my favourites as it involved no homework. He then asked me if I were related to Jim Hume, the lead violinist in the school orchestra. I told him I was indeed. He was a second cousin. He then urged me to learn an instrument and join the school orchestra.

Of course you needed an instrument to join the school orchestra. Jim, a life long friend, had a violin. But musical instruments cost money and we did not have any to spare. That year I also scored the highest mark in maths. I remember I got a perfect score in geometry and a high mark in algebra. Surprising even to me, I found algebra intriguing and really enjoyed solving simultaneous and quadratic equations just for the fun of it.

That year I had a short fictional blurb called "Fantasy" published in the 1948 School Magazine. My cousin Jim Hume, who was a year ahead of me, also had a short piece published. Somehow, I felt that his detracted from mine. But one could never get swelled-headed over a published piece of narrative or a short poem. They did not publish your name, only your initials. Moreover, I had a stern-faced English teacher, a true tyrant, who enjoyed making her pupils feel small. After one class, she called me to her desk to review an essay I had written, pointing out all my mistakes, one of which was spelling travelling with one "L." When she asked me what I intended to do with my life, I told her that I would like to be a writer. She looked at me, sighed, and told me that was very unlikely.

Once in a while I found my way to Jim Hume's house on Henderson Street. One Saturday

I joined him and his father John, to get firewood. There was ten shillings in it for me. John had an old truck and he drove us to some wooded area, handed us axes and we chipped away all morning, until we had a truck full of firewood. On the way back, John stopped at a large home on Great Western Road and went into the house. A few minutes later he came out all smiles for the owner had bought the whole load. And so we went home. I had hoped it would become a regular job. But that was not to be.

By then my mother was going out regularly, every Tuesday and Sunday, with a man called Hughie Gould. They had been introduced by a neighbour, Mrs. Irwin, seemed to get along, and began a longtime relationship. My mother, still young and attractive had been pursued by other men. The landlord's brother for example. A dull fellow. Then there was Stanley, a Polish ex-soldier who was extremely entertaining and could make us all laugh. I once asked him a serious question as to whether there were lions in Poland. Of course, he took advantage of my naivete describing how lions roamed through all the forests of Poland and the like. But it was Hughie who became her regular companion.

Hughie Gould (a posh pronunciation of gold) was aptly named. He had a heart of gold and was always kind and considerate of us. They would usually go to some hotel's salon where, he would have a few drinks. He loved to sing, especially after a drink, and was still ready to sing when he brought my mother home. He sang Scottish songs, Irish songs, even the songs of Al Jolson. Sometimes he coaxed me into singing, but that was rare. While I sang with gusto with my pal Bobby, and even my sister Janice. I had trouble overcoming my shyness with adults.

That summer all the talk in the street was about the Olympic Games, which I wanted dearly to see. Since that was impossible, we street urchins decided to hold our own Olympic games. We mapped out a circuit from Windsor terrace, down Clarendon Street, left on Glenfarg Street, left again on St. Georges Road and left back onto Windsor Terrace. In those days Windsor Terrace extended right to St. Georges Road. We measured out a long jump, a hop skip and jump, a javelin throwing area and so on. I doubt that there were more than five participants. With my long legs, I had an easy victory in the hop, skip and jump. I also had the most endurance in distance running, (probably from running home for dinner) circling the route many times, showing off in front of the girls who gathered around to watch.

Sometime during the year I became

fascinated by magic, in the sense of conjuring. It was incredible to me how magicians could make things appear or disappear. So I became an official member of the Boy Magicians Club. I learned how to lower a piece of loose string into a vase or bottle, say a few magic words, then turn the bottle upside down while keeping the string in place. I learnt to pull out reams and reams of ribbon seemingly out of nowhere. And I learned to do quite a number of card tricks. But I soon realised that to perform the really impressive tricks, you had to practice, practice and practice. I didn't have the time.

I started school again in September, my third form class, called 3B.

I was very interested in astronomy and somehow I learned that, in late October, a comet would pass close to the earth. It was also going to be a particularly good month for spotting meteors. My pal Bobby and I decided that we wanted to enjoy this apparently quite rare opportunity. You could not see much of the sky from a window, or for that matter from anyplace in the street since we were surrounded by tall tenements. So we opted for the easy climb up to the roof of Woodside Halls at the corner of Clarendon and Glenfarg Streets, next to the clinic. And the climb was well worthwhile. Although we had to wait quite late into the night, the clouds were minimal and so we saw a grand display of meteors as well as the comet.

We were on our way home when I realised I had got some dirt on my new jacket. I tried in vain to rub it off. I knew I needed water. We returned to climb on top of the clinic I thought there would be water in there. Nearby was a skylight which opened without any resistance. So we went in. Both expert "dreepers' (we knew how to minimize the fall by lowering yourself until you were only held by a finger) we dropped into the clinic, We could not see much. But when I turned on a light, I quickly found a tap, which I used to clean my jacket. The skylight was above an office area that had a desk which we stood on to get back through the skylight. There were pens and paper and such office stuff on the desk. Since I was badly in need of a pen, I took one and slipped it into my pocket. Just as we were leaving there was a banging on the door and we heard someone yell "police." That sent us scampering to the roof, where we became aware of a couple of policemen who were walking around the building, cutting off our escape route. There was only one recourse. We had to jump from the roof of the clinic onto the roof of another adjacent building and run for it. As the two buildings were separated by a large fence, the police could not follow us. So we jumped.

Once away from the clinic, we raced to

Bobby's house. Bobby cut away and ran up his stairs, while I continued through an underpass right into the arms of a policeman. He had run around and cut me off. He demanded to know where my pal had gone and, getting no response, he punched me in the face breaking my lip. With the threat of more punishment I told him. He also learned that I had taken a pen. Then he took me home advising my mother I would be receiving a summons to court and in the meantime I had to report to the local police station. I went to bed shaken and disgusted with myself.

The following morning was my fifteenth birthday. After I washed and prepared to go to school, my mother pointed to a parcel that was for my birthday. When I opened it, I found it was a new pen. My remorse was indescribable.

When I went to the police station, they took my fingerprints, one by one, by rolling my finger on a pad of black ink, then rolling it on a white pad, leaving a two-dimensional imprint of the contours. I don't recall if I was also photographed, but I understood that I was now, officially, a registered criminal. Afterwards, the policeman took me to a washroom where I washed the ink off my hands.

I was nervous when I was finally called before the court. I had no idea what the punishment would be. I visualized three months in a borstal, twenty lashes, or even time behind bars. I was led to a dock below a bewigged judge who stared down at me from on high. Someone standing beside me spoke to the judge telling him what an exemplary pupil I was, and other kind things. I forget what the judge said, but I was dismissed and told by someone that I had been admonished. That was too big a word for me at that time. But it sounded that I had got away with it. And was I relieved, swearing to myself that I would never allow myself to be in that position again.

My marks in art were deemed good enough to be entered as a contestant in an inter-school art competition. We assembled at the Art Gallery and Museum and told to find a subject and draw it. We were in the natural history section and the choices were bewildering. I finally settled on a goose—I think it was a Canada goose. I laboured all morning before submitting my drawing. My choice proved to be appropriate. I won a goose egg.

The year ended with an Arab attack on Israel, a battle which Israel won. Some called it the great Jewish land grab. It would be the first of many. I subsequently wrote a poem for the school magazine on the difficulties of learning French with the line "He knows it like Arab knows Jew." My English teacher, Mr. MacGregor, liked it but in the end did not publish it.

CHAPTER EIGHTEEN

In my third year at Woodside, I only placed fifth equal in my June examinations. My grades were slipping, my interest waning. The lack of money weighed on my shoulders. I was unable to afford the new school excursions to Switzerland or France. I could not always join my pals when they went to an Italian ice cream parlour, or even buy fish and chips when I was starving. I was rarely able to buy new clothes. I wore my American cousin (Young) Tom's cast-off clothing, sent by Uncle Tom and Aunt May, which looked peculiar for the styles were different from ours. Once they sent me a pair of running shoes. No one had shoes like that in my neighbourhood. However, I liked them for they were very comfortable. But they were also a little too eye-catching for me. Still, I knew it was better than my worn-down leather-soled shoes with the holes in the bottom. Once I tore my trousers, which my mother sewed back together. My mother darned, patched and repaired as best she could. All this served to bring the realization of our poverty to the fore.

My health as usual was not the best. No winter could go by without one, or more colds. These often led to bronchitis which sent me to bed. However, my asthmatic attacks became less frequent. Nevertheless, sometimes there was such a weight on my chest that my mother had to put a hot, very hot, poultice on my chest to break up the flem (phlegm). I would recover, but it cost me days at school where the pace and the demands were increasing.

To earn money I found a job delivering milk in the morning. Like my grocery delivery job, it paid ten shillings a week. I had to get up at 4:30 in the morning, to pick up the bottles of milk, deliver them, and bring back the empties all before breakfast and, of course, before school.

At that time, the transport of milk and bakery items were still performed by a beautiful team of six black horses along a main street like Maryhill Road. They were an awesome sight, for more one had to see a cowboy picture featuring a stage coach to see such a team of horses in action. Of course, they left their mark—a trail of brown earthy dung that really did not smell bad.

Transporting the milk was very different for me. I had a wheel barrow designed for that purpose and I had a schedule telling me where to go and the bottles required. That did not always go smoothly as people would sometimes forget to put out their empty bottles. Also, running up and down stairs was hard work. Inevitably, the lack of sleep made it difficult to focus on my school work and all I had to show for it at the end of the week was a half-a-crown.

It must have increased my appetite. I never seemed to get enough food. Once my mother obtained a bottle of concentrated orange juice, which she kept in the sideboard. I was not aware of it and was just searching for something to eat. Thirsty, I poured some of it into a glass, added water and drank. Like an addict I poured another, then another until it was virtually drained. On another occasion, I found some faux marzipan that my mother had made and devoured most of it, much to her annoyance.

Sometimes my mother and Hughie came home early, or it was some holiday and Hughie would send me for fish and chips. People joke about it being wrapped in newspaper. That is not quite true. The food was placed in a grease-proof bag and then wrapped in newspaper to keep it warm.

I was always delighted with these surprise meals. On really hungry nights, my mother would boil some potatoes with their skins on. With butter, they were a real treat. Then, once in a while, if we had enough sugar—we always traded our sweetie coupons for sugar—she would make hard toffee. It may not have done much for our teeth, but the sweetness and the act of chewing kept the pangs of hunger at bay.

That year, before the start of our summer holidays, a school friend, Sandy Reid, was going to Peebles for a month or so and offered to try and get me to hold down his job of delivering laundry. I got it and loved it. The packages were not only light, the job involved collecting the money which invariably led to a tip. Nothing big, but quite regular. Those I kept along with my usual half-a-crown. I was sorry to have to relinquish it when he returned. I was unable to find anything else.

My mother had a habit of nipping out her cigarettes just before they were finished. She kept these douts (butts) as we called them, at the back of the mantlepiece clock. Though she never explicitly offered them to me, she knew that I looked for them and smoked them. Every day, after dinner and before I went back to school, I would enjoy smoking them and got so addicted that I was in anguish when I found none. This led me to pick up any reasonable sized butt I found on the street. However, this was not enough, and so I picked up every butt I could find, tore away the paper, and pressed the remaining tobacco into a small pipe. Smoking this produced an extraordinary euphoric feeling and left me so light-headed I could barely move. Fortunately, after ten or fifteen minutes, it passed away. Still, I could hardly wait to get home from school to get to my pipe of nicotine. This went on for weeks until I finally realised that this could not be good. Somehow, I managed to quit, though I never stopped smoking.

About that time I think I unloaded my share of sharp-tongued comments, one of which got to my mother so much that she hit me over the head with a dinner plate, smashing it and breaking my scalp. With blood dripping off me, she was forced to apply pressure to stop the bleeding. It was reminiscent of my father. On another occasion, sitting around the fire I said something—I think it was about her visitors keeping me from getting to bed—that she rapped me across the shins with a poker. But my mother was rarely violent, and I understood even then, the burden she bore and the role I had to play for our mutual survival.

Perhaps as a measure of my independence, I began to travel on my own, far and wide. I once took a bus to Campsie Glenn and spent the day there by myself, climbing its steep hill and then, as the sun began to set, running down the hill so fast I was almost flying. Another time I took a streetcar to the Blue Bell woods and walked for miles. Realising it was becoming dark, I returned on a slightly different route and stumbled upon a Gypsies camp, complete with caravans and horses. Some of them stared at me. Thoroughly intimidated, I gave it a wide berth and raced back to the street car terminus. In the colder months, I visited all the museums I could find on the map.

On a Sunday, I used to wander around Barrowland. It was always filled with people often surrounding a cheery hawker— "Not £10, not £5, not £2, just a mere 2/6 and it's yours." Hands went up and the hawker gleefully passed them the merchandise. At that place too, on one corner, you could see a crowd of believers listen to a man preaching about the wrath of God, while on the other corner, an atheist preached on the fallacies of religion. It was all great entertainment.

My first and last experience at a school camp was in the summer of 1949. We stay in an army-type barracks at Lochgoilhead, a little north of Glasgow on the edge of the Grampian Mountains.

It rained every day for two weeks. Nevertheless, one day, my head covered by a sou'wester, I joined the group that climbed the "steeple," and was second man to the top. On another day, I went out for fun in a rowboat with a classmate. But, before long we were fighting for our lives. Unaware that the loch was an arm of the sea, we found ourselves caught by the tide and drifting farther and farther from the shore and we barely moved when we tried to row back. Moreover, a mist had begun to envelop us and visibility was fading fast. We feared that we would be swept unseen into the sea. With the fortitude of true Woodsiders, we concocted a plan whereby one would row with all their strength, until exhausted, at which time the other took over. This way, we inched towards the shore to live another day.

At night, after the lights were turned off, the flashlights came out and the games began. For the most part we played a card game called "brag" where we were dealt three cards and bet according to their value, or your ability to bluff. During one round I was dealt the incredible hand of three jacks. And I bet accordingly. Soon, all but one had thrown in their hand. He matched me bet for bet (all pennies). The boys in the dormitory closed in around us, but they were as quiet as mice. Finally I began to think he may have a better hand, but that would mean he had three queens, three kings or three aces. The odds against this were enormous. But, I finally called him. He had three kings.

*   *   *

In Scotland, at that time, when you reached fifteen years of age, you had the option of leaving school. For sometime I had wondered what kind of job I could do. I remember discussing this with my mother and Hughie. When he asked me what I *wanted* to do, I could only say I did not know. He persisted suggesting that I must have some idea what I wanted to do, until finally I said how can I know what I want to do if I don't know what the job is in the first place. As an analogy I recall saying that "how can you know what a banana tastes like if you haven't tasted a banana." My mother got a bit cross with that, thinking I was being cheeky. I thought I was being perfectly rational.

Finally, after a lot of thought I decided that I could probably be a draftsman. Hughie told me that my apprenticeship might be five years, but that the job paid well and many industries used draftsmen. I was good at maths and excelled in the technical drawing portion of my art class. I had readily grasped the concepts of perspective and vanishing points and could draw a straight line. With this in mind, I left school to enter the world of work. My school provided me with a three-year certificate of merit and wished me well, suggesting, as a first step, I go and see some career consultants.

I thought I would be happy to leave school, but for some reason I wasn't. Nevertheless I dutifully, went downtown to visit a firm of career consultants. I explained my situation, answering some questions as we went along. They thanked me and said to come back at a later date. I was a bit surprised as I expected them to send me to a place that wanted draftsmen. I was even more surprised when I returned.

They told me that it would be inadvisable to leave school, that drafting was not really suitable for me and that I should return to school and aim at being an architect. That certainly gave me something to think about. I was encouraged by their confidence in my ability to do this. I also learned that I was eligible for an annual allowance of some £15, more than enough to buy a new suit and new shoes every year, so long as I continued to go to school.

So, in September of that year, just before my sixteenth birthday, I returned to school to start my fourth year. At this time I was allocated to a class called lV T. Everything was different in the fourth year. The classes had become smaller as people left, and so boys and girls were often in the same class. Moreover, we did not have to line up outside the school anymore and supervision was notably relaxed. If you worked, that was good, if you did not, that was your own responsibility. This atmosphere of trust gave one a sense of dignity. But without the whip (or encouragement) it opened the door to laziness and neglect.

Another significant change was the introduction of options. While you were expected to continue with your studies in English and maths, and must have at least three majors and two minors to graduate with an expectation of going to university, you could add or drop other subjects as you saw fit. Some opted to study another language such as Gaelic or German and so on. I chose English, maths and science for my majors with French and history as my minors, and once again I started school with enthusiasm.

I particularly remember my history class, perhaps because it was full of girls. The boys chose to study geography instead. At the beginning, when asked to read a few chapters of our text book, I sat at home in front of the fire and carefully read every word. When I was back at school, the teacher would ask us questions about the content of the chapters, I had all the answers and my hand always went up. Soon the teacher paid me no regard and tried to elucidate an answer from one of the girls. After that I began to pay less regard myself.

Ireland, the land of my mother's forefathers, became recognized as two distinct entities in 1949, the Republic of Ireland and Northern Ireland which remained a part of Great Britain. My grandfather would have been pleased until the troubles began again.

CHAPTER NINETEEN

The struggle of keeping up continued through the early months of 1950. Now on my way to being seventeen years old, I was ever more acutely aware of my impoverished circumstances. Moreover, I had become so shy it was often painful. I tended to sit at the back of the class out of the way. I went into a sweat when I had to speak in class. Although there were many extracurricular activities that interested me, I could not bring myself to join anything. The girls I knew no longer frequented the streets. We were all too old to play. Moreover, I was so prone to blushing, I would blush even when I had done nothing. I blushed for other people.

Hughie was a generous man. Every Sunday when he came over to take my mother out, he would hand me a fistful of change. All of which went into cigarettes, pictures or snooker. Sometimes I would spend an entire night at the pictures watching two showings with a newsreel or cartoon in between. I watched The Jolson Story six times in a row, going every night for three nights. When I discovered the Gem Theatre was holding a Laurel and Hardy festival, I was there for every show I could afford.

While I was enjoying American, as well as British pictures, an America senator, Joseph McCarthy, began a communist witch hunt that would destroy the careers of many eminent movie actors and directors. Included among these was Larry Parks who so superbly played the role of Jolson. Branded a communist, he became a pariah.

When I was home, I listened to the wireless, "Monday Night at Eight o' clock," "The Man in Black," "Dick Barton—Special Agent," "Saturday Night Theatre" and almost everything else. I even listened to Bernard Shaw's plays on the Third Program. Often I had no choice. I was confined to bed two or three times a winter, always with bronchitis.

Bobby's mother planned to send him off to Australia, but his father, who lived in Luton, stopped it and had him go there. With my friend Bobby gone, I found that I had no real friends at all. For a short time, I palled around with a boy called Kirkwood. His father had hanged himself. There was another time I paid a few visits to Sandy Reid's house and played snooker on a miniature table, but he lived far away and I quickly lost interest. My entire social life revolved around Sam's Snooker Hall. I got to know Sam so well that he allowed me to "poach" on one of the back tables. Poaching was playing, without paying, but playing in the dark. Needless to say, all this took a toll on my grades, though I still went through the motions of writing my weekly essay and other stuff I felt obliged to do. Despite my growing apathy, I somehow garnered enough marks to advance to my fifth year in September.

With no school to worry about, the summer months really dragged. From the library, I would borrow books on astronomy, archeology, mythology, physics (spectrum analysis) and so on, always subjects that I did not get at school. I remember once reading a large book on mythology that kept me occupied for many days to the point that my mother suggested that I spent too much time reading books. "You'll turn your heed into train oil," she said. I never did understand that analogy, but I certainly knew what she meant. I was too old to roam the street and had no special pal, not to mention a girlfriend. I had yet to go on my first date and did not even understand that girls were just as interested in boys as boys were in girls.

It was about this time, after fighting two wars to end all wars, we were again at war, this time in Korea. And, despite already having the deadliest bomb ever invented, the American President Truman authorized the production of the hydrogen bomb—one thousand times more powerful than the atomic bomb. That never sounded too smart to me.

I began my fifth year at high school in class 5B. I had barely started when I came down with a cold. Though away from school only a few days, I was shocked by the speed with which the teachers worked. Some wrote on the blackboard for you to take notes, while all the time talking. When I was not scribbling notes from the board, I was feverishly copying someone else's notes on the lectures I missed. Miss Guy would have been horrified to see how my good penmanship had deteriorated to barely legible wiggling lines. When I got home, I often could not read my own writing.

The teachers had become very tough and demanding. Getting a high mark was always difficult at that school. At times it seemed to be almost impossible. In a page of French dictation, for example, you lost half-a-point for every error, even for a missing grave accent. In an exam, where the marks counted for twenty percent of the course, people had marks worse than zero. Many had scores of minus six or seven or more. Few people got over 70 in any exam.

I had always been somewhat of a quick study. I rarely did any work until it was exam time. For example, I would memorize all the required theorems from my geometry book the night before my exam. Once, someone stole my geometry book, and I had to beg and plead to borrow someone else's. Of course, by this time, we had left Euclidean geometry behind and were studying analytical geometry. Swotting did not work so well, and I paid the price with shocking marks.

I tried to escape by setting an examination to join the Glasgow Corporation, without any preparation, and although I did quite well, I fell short of the cut off mark. I think I was 64th out of some 400 applicants.

To get away, to forget my situation, I would often go to the pictures. Once I travelled across Glasgow to see "Destination Moon." It must have been early in the morning for I recall there were hardly any people in the theatre. Good people work.

I was worn out. I did not feel well. I had

completely lost focus on what I was trying to do. My school marks were dismal. I was fed up relying on people to throw me a tanner or two. When we reached the Xmas holidays, I dropped out of school, this time for good. I was seventeen.

CHAPTER TWENTY

My ambition to write lingered on. So I decided that I should pursue a career in newspaper reporting. To that end, I went to night school to learn Pitman's shorthand, which I thought would be essential for taking notes. Once again, I was a fish out of water. In a class of about twenty, I was the only male. I stuck it out for a few weeks but could not overcome the uncomfortable feeling of being out of place.

Also, I responded to an advertisement in the Glasgow Herald for a laboratory assistant. In my mind, I visualized performing experiments surrounded by test tubes, beakers, microscopes and the like. I thought, with persistence, I could discover cures for ailments and that would make me a famous and valuable person. That night, looking forward to the morning, I started dreaming of the experiments I might conduct. I became very important in my own mind.

When I arrived at the given address, I was surprised to see several relatively small boys, barely fifteen, already waiting to be interviewed for the job. Again, I felt quite out of place and realized the employer's idea of a lab assistant was someone who would sweep the floors. I ran from there as fast as I could.

Directionless, I went back to the career counselors for help in finding a job. They agreed with me and ruled out everything that required some manual labour. I wanted a "white collar" job. After all, despite being 5'11 ' tall, I was not muscular, weighing only about 9 stone or 125 pounds. They wondered if I would be interested in an accounting career. I laughed at that idea for I hated arithmetic. So they sent me to interviews for an office job. I remember being interviewed at Heinz Bean Company. It was too painful for words and got me nowhere.

I became very sick at about this time, literally sick. I was vomiting all over the place. It cleared up only to happen again. Finally, I was sent to the hospital where I was checked out by a doctor and some half-a-dozen students. They pushed and prodded and yattered and yakked until finally coming to the conclusion that I had had food poisoning. I wondered how many times does one have food poisoning, and why was it always only me.

In the interim, my Aunt Mollie arranged for me to meet a relation of hers who had connections that might be useful to me. I recall that he had a box attached to his mantlepiece which held cigarettes. He pushed some button and out popped a cigarette, which he lit with a fancy lighter. I was impressed with his sophistication. Though I was dying for a smoke, he never offered me one. I felt that he did not interview me as much as he talked about himself. I never heard from him again.

Later, one of my career counselors arranged for me to meet a man in the Civil Service who might be able to get me a job. This interview I vividly recall. I sat in front of his desk and stammered my every answer. I was so embarrassed at my own inarticulate responses that my face turned crimson. I could not wait to get away. Later, the career counsellor told me they got a letter from the man. It contained just one word. No!

In June of 1950, I slipped into Woodside Halls, only a stone's throw from my home in

Windsor Terrace, to watch my schoolmates receive their school prizes. With a sad and heavy heart, I watched unseen at the back of the hall. Most of them would go on to attend university, and I felt sick at my failure to do so.

As usual, Norman Coutts took most of the prizes. He went on to be a doctor. Another schoolmate went on to be a reporter. Another friend, Ian Grant, went to London to be a customs officer, but not before he coaxed me into joining the FP (Former Pupils) Club, where I played table tennis. Another went on to be an actuary. Yet another, an engineer. I could only wonder what I would go on to be.

Meanwhile, my counselors sent me to William H. Jack and Company, a firm of Incorporated Accountants at 49 Bath Street. Fortunately, it had nothing to do with accounting. They wanted a rent collector and I was it. I think that my size seemed to be the determining factor. The average height for a Scottish man in those times was around 5' 6" to 5"8". In addition, my boss to be, Mr. Kilpatrick was rarely in the office. This was the property management division of the Company, and he apparently spent a lot of time visiting potential customers. My job was to periodically knock on doors to collect the rent. It was in a slum district, but when some of the people invited me in, I was often amazed at how clean and cared for many of the homes were. Often I came back with pockets full of pound notes, which I deposited in the firm's account in the bank downstairs. There was complete trust. I remember being amazed at the bank balance.

The secretary there, Elizabeth Kilday, was about sixty years old, yet we immediately became good friends. Indeed, I got on well with everyone. In the mornings, when I was not out, I was often assigned to get some hot buttered scones, while they made the tea. This was work?

I was hired at the incredible wage of £2 per week. Of course, I gave all my earnings to my mother who gave me back 10 shillings. With this improvement in my income, I was able to buy a full pack of Players cigarettes, a copy of the Reveille, and go to the pictures every week. Also every Saturday night I went to another snooker hall, classier than Sam's, and proudly paid my way. While I was usually broke by the following Wednesday or Thursday, I took comfort in the fact I would get another 10 shillings on the Friday. Life could not be better.

But again I became sick. This time the pain became unbearable. I went to bed, tossing about with the pain. It was Sunday night that Hughie regularly took my mother out. They gave me an

184

Askit (aspirin) and left me to sleep. Still the pain increased and I vomited all over the floor at the side of my bed, a green, vile vomit. By the time my mother came back, around midnight, I was writhing around the bed in agony. It surprised me that her eyes fell first to the ugly mess on the floor asking me why I could not have been sick in a basin or something. I said I could not help it.

By this time I was beginning to go into shock. I recall moaning about the tingling in my nose as I rocked about. Hughie said he would go to a chemist for something to help. Since it was now after midnight, he had to take a street car downtown to Boots the Chemist. Though it seemed like an eternity, he finally returned with some medicine that stopped the pain and calmed me down. Exhausted, I soon fell asleep.

The following morning Dr. Reid, who lived across the street, came to see me. As I lay on the bed, he pressed around my stomach until I yelped in pain. I must have fallen asleep again, for the next thing I remember was being strapped into a stretcher and carried downstairs to an ambulance. Fifteen minutes after I arrived at the hospital, I was taken to the operating room. I remember them placing some thick socks on my feet, nothing more.

I awoke in a hospital bed, minus my appendix. I learned later that I narrowly missed peritonitis, as the appendix broke during the operation. Indeed, the straight line incision turned to the left making the cut on my stomach somewhat unusual.

A week later, I was out of hospital, and a week after that, to everyone's surprise, I was back playing table tennis on Friday night at the Woodside FP Club. I started work on the following Monday. Many weeks later, probably late August, to my absolute amazement, one the partners of the firm, I think his name was Caldwell, arranged for me to go to a convalescent home in East Kilbride for two weeks at no cost. Moreover, my weight had gone up to almost ten stone (about 136 lbs.).

Since I was no longer sick, it turned out to be one of the most enjoyable holidays I ever had. The convalescents were a mixture of old and young, male and female. The nurses were all young, many at about my age. I became friendly with one in particular mainly because she could play the piano. We all got together at night for a singsong and many sang songs on their own. We all went on a bus ride where we sang again. Off the bus, we walked around the dunes.

Towards the end of my time there, I met a young pretty girl with whom I fell in love. It was the first time I felt such a powerful emotional attraction. She was an Irish girl named May McVey.

Her hair was a dark reddish colour and, in the sun, it shone like gold. On top of that, she had dazzling green eyes. She seemed amenable to me and we went for walks together. Sometimes several of us went out together and on the way wanted to stop for some tea and a bun, if not more. I had long since spent my allowance. Desperate for money, I wrote to my mother begging her to send me a pound or so. She did send me ten shillings with which I was able to pick up the tab for everyone, once. Then it was gone.

During our walks, I learned that May was a Catholic, apparently not a good thing for me, a Protestant, though I truly did not understand this division, which in time brought me to seriously question the validity of any religion. I learned she lived in Greenock and was even more naive about life than me. We had barely any physical contact— only an occasional light kiss. Nevertheless, I was seriously heartbroken when my time there came to an end, and we had to part. So powerful was my attachment to her that it took five years for me to get over her. For months I moped about the house thinking of her, even weeping when I heard a certain song on the wireless. Once, I took a bus to Greenock and walked about the streets in the pouring rain hoping that I would see her. I was never to see her again.

My mother had no idea how distraught I was. And, I could not tell her. All the exchange of confidences in my family took place between my mother and sister. In truth, when not otherwise occupied, my sister spent her time sitting on her mother's knee. This was not only when she was an infant, but when she was nine, ten, eleven and even twelve. Their close relationship did not fundamentally change until my sister left home at nineteen. For me there was little warmth. Perhaps it is different with boys, but I cannot recall a single time in my childhood that my mother gave me a pat on the head, never mind a hug. She appeared blissfully unaware of her indifference.

That October I became eighteen. It was not special to me. However, my mother thought that it gave me justification to ask for a rise (raise) in pay. I was mortified at the thought. I had hardly started. Still, my mother insisted that it was normal practice and I did not know better. Somehow I dredged up the courage, or gall, to inform Mr. Jack of the change in my age. Then I spluttered out that I wondered if I could get a rise in pay. He spared me his shock and said that he would think about it. The following Friday, when I opened my pay packet, it had half-a-crown extra.

Several weeks later, we learned that we would be able to emigrate to Canada. My Uncle

Tom, Aunt Jean and Uncle Willie all contributed the money for our fare. Now we had to get passports and be cleared by the Canadian emigration officials. This required a medical and a birth certificate. One Sunday night, with Hughie on hand, my mother gave me my birth certificate. It was only then I realized I was an illegitimate child and my legal name was Ernest Moore. I was shocked to the core.

My mother explained that my father had been married before and couldn't get a divorce before my birth. She said they had tried to have my name changed, but that it could not be done under Scottish law. She also had a letter that verified their attempt to change the name on my birth certificate. This was all news to me. Hughie asked me if I understood that it was just a matter of fate. With some bravado, I proclaimed that it didn't matter to me at all, and no more was ever said about it. Fifty years would pass before I learned, quite by accident, that my father had another child, a girl called Jean. So, unknown to me for most of my life, I had an older half-sister.

When I received my passport it bore the name Ernest Moore Hume. With the latter name being underlined. Regardless, it would get me into Canada. (Years later, I did what they could not or would not be bothered doing. I had my surname legally changed to Hume).

Knowing now that I would soon be going to Canada, I began to let others know, especially my friend Bobby Campbell. Bobby had come back to his mother's house for a spell with the intention of joining the navy. After her divorce or separation, his mother had married, or chose to live with, a man called Maxwell, which probably led to the idea of shipping Bobby off to Australia. Maxwell liked to play cards, so for a while, we got together every Sunday. I quite enjoyed these visits, for I usually won. When I announced I would soon be sailing to Canada, Maxwell warned me about how rough the Atlantic could be, especially in the winter and how sick I would be. I had not thought of that. "You could face forty-foot waves" he said enjoying my consternation. I still left with all the money.

Although eighteen, I had never had a girlfriend, though I had many girl acquaintances, the closest being Ruth Hall who I had begun sitting with, in front of her fireplace on Saturday nights—with Bobby by my side. I am sure she liked me. However, I felt no passion for her like that I had felt for May. I was completely uneducated in matters of sex and knew of no way to find out. I had only my instincts as a guide. I also was aware that I would soon be called up to join the army, though I had decided that, if necessary, I would choose the air force. The other alterative was the navy which was so popular that you had to sign up for five years as Bobby did.

Then the speed of events almost overpowered me.

*   *   *

I received short notice that there was a last minute cancellation for a berth on R.M.S. Franconia. This was Cunard's second liner with that name built by John Brown's Shipyard. In 1938, it was refitted as a troopship. During WW ll, she took part in the evacuations of Norway and France and the invasion of Sicily, and served as the headquarters ship at Yalta. In 1949, the Franconia returned to Cunard's service on the Canada routes from Liverpool. It seemed fitting to me that I would be transported across the Atlantic on a ship built by the people of Clydebank.

I was to sail from Liverpool to Halifax on December 1, 1951, and then take a 27-hour train trip to Montreal to be met by my Aunt Jean. My mother and sister were to follow in the new year. When I got there, my first objective was to get a job and send the money back to my mother, after paying my aunt for my room and board.

Breaking the news to my employer William H. Jack was extremely difficult. They were so kind and fair to me, first by giving me employment at all, then by sending me on a holiday to recuperate, when I felt perfectly well, and then giving me an uncalled for increase in my pay. They even gave me a parting reference to help me get a job in Canada. All this for a few months of service.

Over the years, my propensity for collecting bits and pieces of nature's produce enabled me to create a small museum. Chief among these items was the skeleton of a frog, not one of mine. Before I left for Canada, I donated all these items to Mrs. Smith, Leslie's mother, who was an elementary school teacher, and she was most grateful.

We had been warned that the winters were very cold in Canada. So, before I left, I got a new winter coat, a Crombie, and a long sought-after hat. I packed all my clothes into a medium-size suitcase and carried eight Canadian dollars for my out-of-pocket expenses.

My mother, sister and Aunt Mollie saw me to Central Station to catch the train to Liverpool. The parting was uneventful other than the fact that my well-intentioned aunt asked the people in the carriage I climbed into to keep an eye on me. Humiliated yet again, I mumbled something about not needing any help and was glad when the train pulled away from the station.

I boarded the ship and found my cabin on the

lower decks. There was already an occupant there lying on the lower bunk bed, He was Irish, enjoyed hurling and had wrists twice as thick as mine, but through the whole voyage, he was never able to leave the cabin for seasickness.

Not I. I went to the cabin only to sleep, and then not always. A few days out, we were struck with gale force winds. The ship rolled like a drunken sailor. The wind ferociously whipped up the sea. Whitecaps were everywhere.

I stood by the rail facing the wind and watched the water climb high on the ship's side and then fall to the bottom, about forty feet, I thought. Across that frantic water, lay the land of my birth, the schools that had opened my mind and the room where I had spent half of my life. I could not restrain the tears. I thought about the last verse of the Woodside School song:

> *So may we on the tide of time*
> *Send ringing out to sea*
> *Fortitudine, Fortitudine,*
> *Fortitudine, Vincemus.*

And my spirits soared, and I was filled with hope.
Bring it on world! I roared.
Bring it on!

www.ingramcontent.com/pod-product-compliance
Lightning Source LLC
Chambersburg PA
CBHW060651150426
42813CB00052B/671